**PRINT CASEBOOKS 9/
THE BEST IN EXHIBITION DESIGN**

PRINT CASEBOOKS 9

THE BEST IN EXHIBITION DESIGN

Written by **Edward K. Carpenter** Published by **RC Publications, Inc. Rockville, MD**

Introduction

PRINT CASEBOOKS 9/THE BEST IN EXHIBITION DESIGN (1991-92 EDITION)
Library of Congress Catalog Card Number 75-649581
ISBN 0-915734-73-7

PRINT CASEBOOKS 9 (1991-92 EDITION)
Complete 6-Volume Set
ISBN 0-915734-69-9
3-Volume Set No. 1 ISBN 0-915734-76-1
3-Volume Set No. 2 ISBN 0-915734-77-X

RC PUBLICATIONS
President and Publisher: Howard Cadel
Vice President and Editor: Martin Fox
Art Director: Andrew P. Kner
Managing Director: Linda Silver
Consultant: Teresa Reese

Institutional changes affecting art and science museums continue unabated. Not only are more of these museums being built, but long-existing ones are receiving facelifts, and their exhibits are being presented in fresh ways. It is no longer enough for a museum to put out phalanxes of rocks or bones or oil paintings from 17th-century Florence with labels telling what they are. It is necessary now to provide information explaining the reason for their importance, their place in the culture from which they came, and their significance for the viewer. All this is a challenge for the exhibit designer, who must show items in contexts much more complicated than was once favored by museums.

Yet, contradictory as it seems, the evidence shows that as exhibits become more complicated, they are, in a way, becoming simpler, too. Instead of the ideal being to display everything in a museum's collection at once, the emphasis now is on the quality of display—on perhaps showing fewer items but presenting them more clearly, in ways that make people want to experience them. A current ideal would be to display each item so that it can be seen completely and freshly, so that it stands out and is shown off. Exhibit designers are putting as much thought into preparing the lighting, the background, the supports, and the labeling for each item in an exhibit as a movie crew does in setting up a star for a close-up. As a result, many once-musty exhibits are now sparkling and alive.

Nowhere are these changes as pronounced as in zoos and aquariums. Long in the process of releasing their land animals from iron-barred prisons, or water dwellers from sterile tanks, into environments approximating those the creatures would inhabit in the wild, these institutions are beginning to see themselves as a source of information about the importance of the interrelationship of all life. They are beginning to share that information actively. In line with this, zoos are setting themselves up as the keepers of endangered species, hoping that as the swelling hordes of mankind continue to despoil the world, species that would otherwise disappear forever can be kept alive in zoos. They even see themselves as the carriers of the message that we cannot kill off other species—whether algae, trees, or whales—without destroying ourselves, too. Their medium for this message is exhibits. For the first time, permanent zoo and museum exhibitions are becoming a widespread alternate source of essential information that the schools, and the media—films, books, magazines, newspapers, and even television—often cannot convey with the same immediacy.

None of these changes has come easily, without dissent or disruption. There are those who are reluctant to see institutions change from being warehouses or jails to being teachers of the masses. Then there are the inevitable disputes about the level of education these institutions should provide. Should it be democratic, aimed at everyone equally, or only at ignoramuses or scholars? The dispute also concerns whether learning should be fun and, if so, just what constitutes fun. The International Journal of Museum Management and Curatorship editorializes about what it sees as the "trivialization" of collections and the spiritual decline of museums. But at least one museum administrator, George F. MacDonald of the Canadian Museum of Civilization in Ottawa, points out the painfully obvious when he notes that the average museum visitor in North America stays less than an hour and leaves with museum fatigue, while visitors to Epcot Center at Walt Disney World stay eight hours and leave refreshed. At Epcot, he says, "visitors are alternatively entertained, fed, educated, and given souvenirs."

Charles P. Reay, who designed the exhibits in the Living World at the St. Louis Zoo, speaks of the "new responsibilities" these institutions must confront. He argues that zoos can no longer be limited merely to describing zoology: "It is critical for them to move beyond their myopic and parochial view of things if they are to succeed in meeting their new responsibilities." They need to make those "critical connections," he says, between the display of animals and the revelation of ideas and forces that control our lives. In the exhibits he designed for Living World, Reay, who is a senior vice-president of the St. Louis architectural firm Hellmuth, Obata and Kassabaum, goes a long way toward showing how exhibits can make this leap, from being

mere displays to being what he calls "places of wonder and awe that celebrate life and discovery—and beauty and connections—and how in nature all things fit." In a way he's saying what violinist Isaac Stern used to say about the difference between merely playing the notes and making those notes sing. Reay would hope that zoo exhibits can come to sing touchingly enough to instill in visitors, not just an understanding of, but a love for, the workings and wonder of life on earth, a love "strong enough to bring about that change in personal priority" needed if we are going to survive.

Reay's exhibit uses almost all the devices currently available to exhibit designers to make the zoo's message sing. Its message is intelligently presented without frivolity or folderol, offering something for a toddler who will delight in watching a quail hatch from its egg or a hamster snuggling with its siblings, and offering something, too, to the college student who wants to know about the sensory perception of a fish's lateral line or a honey bee's third, fourth, and fifth eyes. It is interesting to note that the HOK-designed Living World increased the St. Louis Zoo's attendance from 2,200,000 a year where it had fallen from a peak of 2,700,000 in 1986, to 3,000,000 in the year after the new facility opened.

Of the 26 exhibits discussed here, 11 are science exhibits and only seven are art exhibits, if we don't count architecture, industrial design, or set design (each represented by a single exhibit) as art.

Two of the science exhibits are aquariums, a special design category whose designers have to deal with a welter of hoses, pumps, aerators, heaters, coolers, holding tanks, drains, water pipes, and vitrines (tanks) that cloud up with algae and have to be cleaned regularly.

One exhibit is a gallery in the Indianapolis Children's Museum that was designed by the young people who use it. The gallery, known as the Center for Exploration, became a place where children gather regularly and frequently to do such things as compose music on synthesizers, develop computer programs, read, hang out, make videos, paint murals, and choreograph dance routines. Some of what they produce is displayed in the gallery, but, whatever the results of these activities, the Center for Exploration is carrying the Museum into new areas. It is definitely not just a place where items of interest to children are kept and occasionally taken out and displayed behind glass. It is now a place where children learn by doing.

Two of the exhibits discussed here deal with Japan. As might be expected with exhibits influenced by a Japanese esthetic, both are examples of a spare, quiet exhibit design that allows a visitor to see each item set off exquisitely against just the right colored and textured backdrop, lighted to show off its every facet and given enough space to be experienced individually.

But this spareness and calm is not just the province of the Japanese. Other exhibits in these pages fit the same mold.

Two of them deal with Western art. One is Val Lewton's design for the Louis Comfort Tiffany exhibit at the National Museum of Art's Renwick Gallery, and the other is ElRoy Quenroe's reinstallation of the permanent collection at the Walters Art Gallery in Baltimore. When Quenroe finished with the Walters, he says, curators told him they were noticing things about some of the art on exhibit that had escaped their notice before.

There is, of course, another approach used in exhibits to attract and hold attention, one that is noisy, cluttered, and filled with bright, clashing colors. Visual clutter is a form of stress and, I am sure, a leading cause of museum fatigue. But in an era when television with its quickly changing images, and bright colors, is the prime esthetic model for youngsters, children quickly become bored with anything else. Their frenetic energy is too often picked up by adults. Our national attention span seems to be 30 seconds, after which we need to quick-cut to something else. Visual clutter is, of course, everywhere; it is pervasive enough to sustain an argument that it has become our national esthetic. You don't have to watch television or step into a trade show to be convinced. You have to look no further than the strip you drive past or the mall where you shop. look around you at the mall.

But at times this clutter has charm. The one trade exhibit in these pages is the "Aggression Is Our Obsession" show that O'Neill Inc.'s design department did to attract attention to the firm's line of wet suits and sportswear. Its wit and joy are as obvious as its stridency. Stridency is, of course, the point. According to the current wisdom, to be noticed at a trade show, an exhibit has to shout louder than its competitors. But what if someone designed a calm, uncluttered, visually non-aggressive trade show—one that called attention to itself by the purity of its design and the serenity of its presence? Someone did, in fact, design such a show, though it wasn't built on a noisy trade convention floor. Vanderbyl Design designed it to display Esprit's line of shoes, belts, and handbags to professional buyers at the Esprit showroom in New York's Rockefeller Center.

As usual, we have examples of fine exhibit design done on all sorts of budgets, from the $7500 that Bower Leet Architects raised for their "Constructing Light" exhibit at Parsons School of Design to the $4.5 million the Franklin Institute spent on the exhibits for its Futures Center.

What the jurors for this Casebook were seeking, as they reviewed slides of almost 200 exhibits to select the 26 shown here, were examples of innovation. They did not, they said, want to see just a good traditional exhibit. They wanted something different. And though at a time when so much of an exhibit's content may be on a laser disk or a video screen, or in the invisible intricacies of a computer program, they found what they were after.

About half (maybe slightly fewer) of these exhibits use computers, and in each of these the computer is more than an adjunct to the exhibit; it is integrated into its fabric. Nowhere is the exhibit hidden within the computer and the exhibit framework merely a device to attract the visitor to the computer. It is as if designers are becoming comfortable with computers (and the video screen) and are finding ways of using them as the supporting tools they are instead of trying to let them be the show itself.

Exhibit designers continue to come from a host of backgrounds. Perhaps this diversity of experience keeps them from foundering on the rocks of fad and formality, and may help to explain the freshness in the look of today's exhibits. And the lack of ground rules, written or unwritten, means designers are more likely to take creative chances. We can't show you the hauntingly beautiful electron microscope film of a honey bee that Chip Reay and David Scharf put together for the Living World at the St. Louis Zoo, but you can get an idea of what visitors see at "Whales: Giants of the Deep," the exhibit that Daniel Quan designed for the Pacific Science Center in Seattle. You can become acquainted, too, with some of the Living World and, of course, 24 other exhibits, each of them special in its own way.
—*Edward K. Carpenter*

Edward K. Carpenter

For many years an editor with national architectural and design magazines, Edward K. Carpenter writes extensively in both fields. He is the author of books on urban design, environmental design and industrial design, as well as exhibition design. This is his eighth *Exhibition Design Casebook*.

Dextra Frankel

As a full professor at California State University in Fullerton, Dextra Frankel teaches in a program that leads to a Master's degree in exhibition design. Hers is one of the few programs in the country offering a degree—let alone courses—in exhibition design. Through her teaching, and through her own work, her influence on the profession is widespread. Her own exhibition design, which she has practiced since 1967 as director of the Art Gallery at the California State University, Fullerton, has won many awards. Her firm, Dextra Frankel Associates, in Culver City, CA, specializes in exhibition design. In 1978, Frankel received a grant from the National Endowment for the Arts to study and work in Japan. In 1985, another NEA grant allowed her to travel in Western Europe.

John A. Gwynne, Jr.

In 1986, John Gwynne became deputy director for design of the New York Zoological Society, responsible for all its buildings and design. He took on the job when the Society's aquarium, botanical garden, and zoos were undergoing extensive and long-term changes, bringing to the assignment a broad background in horticulture, exhibition design, graphics, and illustration. Since receiving a Master's degree in landscape architecture from Harvard in 1974, Gwynne has been involved with zoos and parks, specializing in designing and interpreting wild areas for an urban public. From 1975 to 1977, he was director of exhibits and graphics at the Roger Williams Park Zoo in Providence, RI, and after a five-year stint as the acting director of development and environmental services for the Providence Department of Public Parks, Gwynne moved to the New York Zoological Society in 1982 as curator of exhibits and graphics. Throughout a career in which he also was a consultant in zoo and landscape design, Gwynne built an international reputation as an illustrator of field guides.

Edwin Schlossberg

As president, principal designer, founder, and owner of the 40-member design firm Edwin Schlossberg, Inc., Edwin Schlossberg is the developer and designer of all the firm's projects. These include interactive museum exhibits, entertainment centers, and information systems. Schlossberg, who has a Ph.D. in Science and Literature from Columbia University, has taught college courses and lectured and written widely. He was a lecturer in MIT's urban planning department and Columbia's arts administration program, and he was artist-in-residence at the University of Illinois/Urbana. His most recent book, which he co-authored, is *Teaching Children to Think Like Animals: The Macomber Farm Project.*

Stephanie Tevonian

In 1988, after 8½ years as a partner in the New York City design firm Works, Stephanie Tevonian set up her own firm, Stephanie Tevonian Design, which designs books, graphics, signs, and exhibitions. She says the philosophy of the graphic design program at Yale, where she earned a Master of Fine Arts degree, was that once designers learned the design process and how to solve a graphic design problem, they could probably design "most anything." She had a chance to test this philosophy when Works moved from two-dimensional graphic design into three-dimensional signs and exhibits. Twice Tevonian hosted an annual program for the American Institute of Graphic Arts in New York called "Not Flat (design)." One of her recent exhibit designs was a traveling exhibit, "Hot Circuits: A Video Arcade," which she designed for New York's American Museum of the Moving Image.

Index

The Eli Lilly Center for Exploration

The Eli Lilly Center for Exploration at the Children's Museum in Indianapolis is a 15,000-sq.-ft. gallery where the youngsters who use it—limited to ages 10 to 18—create some of the exhibits that it displays. In an effort to attract more adolescents, whose attendance had dwindled, the museum offered 10- to 18-year-olds their own space, free from the presence of parents and tots. But there is much more to the story.

The museum wanted not only to lure adolescents but also to hold them. It wanted them to make a commitment to using the museum more than a couple of hours once a year or even once a month. It wanted them to come in frequently, daily perhaps, and stay and help, to become part of the museum and its programs.

What developed out of this desire carried the museum down a path that may seem landscaped with elements of daycare, or neighborhood center, or arts-and-crafts camp. But the physical design and programs that emerged are undeniably more sophisticated than any of these. The result is, at its core, a museum exhibition space for adolescents that owes its success to the museum staff, 10 or 15 of whom initiated the idea, and hundreds of kids who helped with the design.

The actual concept for the gallery came from three museum staffers: Kay Harmless, who joined the museum as director of the Center for Exploration while it was still only a gleam in the museum's collective eye; Ann Ray, a computer education specialist who was to become one of the Center's master teachers, and Tina Sibbitt, the

museum's exhibit design group leader. All of them are experienced in working with children, and they devised a program to involve children in the design of an exhibit gallery. They were as interested in the process as in the result, and a key to the process is that they hired three adolescents to be the actual designers of the gallery.

These three had all been finalists in one of the museum's yearly art competitions. Although none of them had any design training, Sibbitt felt that teaching these artists to become designers should be part of the process. They would test their designs by putting them out for the scrutiny of the youngsters who visited the museum. "I wanted the [designer] kids to listen to what their peers were saying, to get outside input, so they would

produce a design that would appeal as widely as possible." In short, she wanted them to approach exhibit design the way a professional would.

For the young designers to accept a team approach, Sibbitt says, was the hardest part of the project. However, in three intense months, with Sibbitt's guidance, the teenage designers produced what were, if not finished designs, at least design suggestions for the gallery. There were even design drawings for some of the details. Then, summer vacation over, they went back to school and Sibbitt stepped in to refine and implement their designs "as honestly as possible. I detailed and specified all designs for the gallery," she says.

What emerged was a design that Sibbitt hopes represents the Center for Exploration's basic concept: "that it should

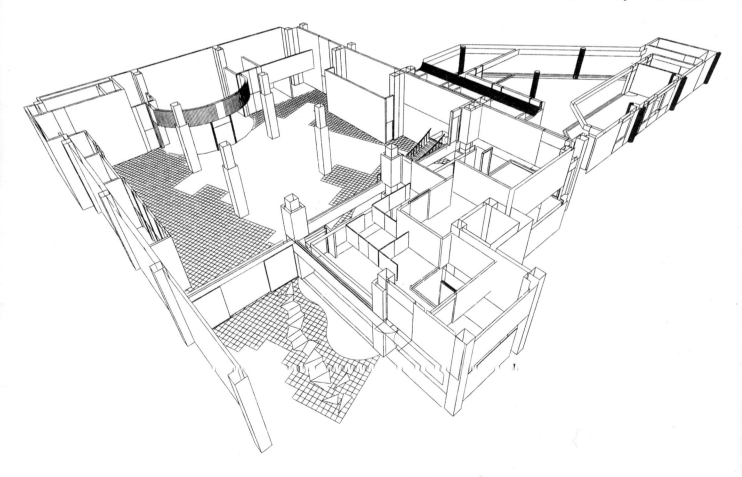

engage youth and encourage them to become explorers." Perhaps it is still too soon to tell whether the design can do all that's expected of it. But the concept seems to have worked for the three teenage designers: All have gone on to design school.

In the center's 15,000 sq. ft. are at least seven distinct areas. Off a central gallery area are:

Arts area. Here, kids can get hands-on experience in a number of techniques, including airbrushing, silkscreening, and painting. There is a darkroom, with teacher, open every day. At one time, there were paper-making sessions. Kids collected lint, made papier-mâché, and glued it to an 8'-by-60' canvas, creating a mural depicting environmental needs. It is now on display in the museum.

*Resource center (*quiet area*).*

The kids call this space "data base" and in it are books and magazines and comfortable seating so they can sit and read or look at slides and videos. There is also a copying machine, and there is talk of trying to get a public library branch to come into the space.

Carpentry shop. A carpenter shows up every day to show kids how to use woodworking tools and machines and help them make things.

Theater. Using this mirror-lined space, youngsters, with the help of the Butler University dance program, choreographed and performed their own creation, "Trash Dance." The area has a sound system and theatrical lights hanging from a yellow truss.

On a mezzanine overlooking the gallery are:

Media laboratory (music, video, and computers). Seven

personal computers are set up here. One of the Center's master teachers shows kids how to work programs and helps them create their own. The computers are capable of desktop publishing, and kids have turned out pamphlets and brochures. This section also has a custom-designed table for music equipment. For the first six months after the Center opened, a musician came in and showed the kids how to use and to write music for a synthesizer. In the video part of the area, donated by TV host David Letterman, an Indianapolis native, kids can put together their own videos, producing and editing them.

Studio area. "Studio" is the name assigned a complex of mezzanine rooms containing two offices, a conference room, a snack area, and studio space around a central work area.

Glass walls separate the rooms from the central seating area and its floor pattern of blue, black, and white tiles.

Children's Express area. This is the room for the Center's newspaper, produced by the youngsters themselves.

Typical of the way the designers worked was their color selection process. To find out the color preferences of the children who would use the Center for Exploration, the designers laid out color swatches on a central table at the museum. After tabulating preferences, they found—not surprisingly—that kids like vivid colors: bright blues, violets, reds, and greens. Though the designers used modifications of these colors, not copying them exactly, they had learned what their clients liked. Throughout the Center, the basic color scheme is black and white with

1. Isometric drawing of Center for Exploration.
2. Brushed stainless steel path leads through gallery space. Visitors stare into anti case which holds such un-museum-like artifacts as a red Harley Davidson motorcycle. Above anti case is room where museum visitors put out Children's Express newspaper.
3. Neon rings wrap top of freestanding column with black-and-white graphics by teenage designers.

11/Exhibition Design

2. 3.

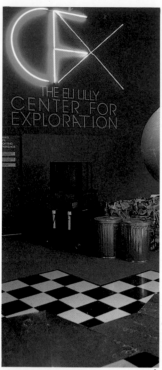

yellow accents. Tomato red, turquoise, blue-violet, chartreuse, and Mediterranean blue also appear.

Visitors enter the Center for Exploration on a black-and-white checkerboard floor of 12"-square tiles whose history also illustrates how the young designers operated. The designers had sought a device to separate the center visually from the rest of the museum. On a trip to Chicago's Merchandise Mart, they crossed a black-and-white checkered floor that gave them "a feeling they were floating" on it. They stopped and asked questions. Then, back in Indianapolis, they incorporated a somewhat similar floor of vinyl composition tile into their design. It runs on a diagonal into and through the 8000-sq.-ft. gallery space that is the heart of the Center. Set into the

floor is a brushed stainless steel path that gives an illusion of depth. The remainder of the gallery floor is exposed concrete.

In the open space are four freestanding columns painted with black and white graphics designed by the kids and wrapped at their top with neon rings. Overhead, red industrial fluorescent fixtures contrast with the blue-purple ceiling. Tina Sibbitt designed the Center's lighting, using both fluorescent and incandescent track lighting arranged in three individually controlled sections.

On the gallery's perimeter are storage rooms faced with marker board on which current events or anything else can be noted. Higher up is space for murals or canvas banners (up to 15' long, set in an aluminum track) on which graphics can be painted. The designers covered

some wall surfaces with Eurotex wall carpeting to which they can apply Velcro graphics or labels.

Just inside the entrance is a display case (26' long by 7' high by about 30" deep) earmarked to hold items that would excite adolescent visitors. The usual stuff in the museum's cases, the designers thought, was too dull, not cool. Known as the "anti case," it holds a stuffed flamingo and a plastic one, a human skeleton with sun glasses, a dog skeleton, a fish tank with live fish, and a red Harley-Davidson motorcycle.

The filtration system of the anti case's fish tank is exposed, in line with the decision for the center to symbolize a "transparency of ideas." Toward this end, almost everything—ducts, pipes, girders—is left exposed. Says Tina Sibbitt, "The gallery has a

4.

5.

6.

very hard-edged, dramatic feel."

The Casebook jurors liked the Center's utility and immediacy. "Real," they called it, and "strong."

Design and production of the Center for Exploration took 18 months on a budget of $1,000,000, 10 per cent of which went for computers, video, and musical equipment.

7.

8.

4. Center for Exploration logo above entrance.
5. Artifacts in anti case are not those usually found in museum cases. Note reclining skeleton and stuffed flamingoes.
6. Fractal wall graphic designed by adolescent designers in Center's Media Lab. Video music equipment is in front of graphic.
7. Visitors wear CFX T-shirts in Video Room.
8. Children's Express newspaper office.
9. Computers on gallery floor.
10. Gallery space with wall graphics and murals designed by children who use the museum.

9.

10.

Client: The Children's Museum (Indianapolis, IN)
Sponsor: The Eli Lilly Co.
Design firm: The Children's Museum
Designers: Tina Sibbitt (Children's Museum staff), Kris Cerola, Auriea L. Harvey, Martina Nehrling
Fabricators: The Children's Museum; Paul D. Metals (stainless steel floor)

Space: The Next Generation

"Space" was the first exhibit organized for the newly opened Center for Exploration (CFX) at the Children's Museum in Indianapolis, Indiana (see preceding story.), and it was meant as a prototype. But because of its size, it wouldn't fit in the Center's gallery space, so it was designed, instead, to fit the Children's Museum's Spurlock Special Exhibitions Gallery (9000 sq. ft.), which is next to the CFX gallery. In fact, part of the CFX mezzanine overlooked the first exhibit.

Like all projects at the Children's Museum, "Space" grew out of the work of a staff team, this time with three members: exhibit designer Steven W. Sipe; the director of the Center for Exploration, Kay Harmless; and one of the Center's master teachers, Ann Ray. They spent two days consulting with a group of 20 children, 10 of whom were junior high school students; five, elementary school students; and five, high school students. Asked by the staff team what they would like in a space exhibit, the children said they wanted to see an exhibit of what's ahead in space flight and, maybe, some of what's going on now. They wanted to know about U.S. plans for a space station, about future colonization and advanced work at NASA. They wanted to be told how they could get into the program. What they didn't want was a history of space flight. That was old hat.

The museum team then met for a couple of days with an advisory group of 25 or 30 individuals from NASA and from schools and universities. Finally, the team visited U.S. space and rocket centers in Houston, Texas, and Huntsville, Alabama.

Exhibit designer Sipe set the mood by filling the windows in the gallery's curved exterior wall with a couple of dozen backlit blowups, either 4' by 4' or 3' by 3', of color transparencies of planets, stars, and nebulae. The CFX's mezzanine overhangs the first third or so of this gallery, limiting the ceiling to 9'. But beyond that, the ceiling opens to 22', and Sipe filled the space with models of NASA hardware, in some cases close to full scale. He had, for instance, a full-scale reconstruction of the space shuttle's cargo bay (12' by 26' and about 9' tall) fabricated of welded aluminum ribs and a skin of white vinyl. He also had a simulation of the space shuttle's living spaces and flight deck built to full scale (12' by 14' and about 16' high) of plywood and studs with a Masonite skin. From the shuttle living area, visitors could pass through a simulated airlock to an aluminum-ribbed, vinyl-fabric-covered mockup of the proposed space station Freedom's habitability module. Built about 9' high, 12' wide, and 36' long, just 4' short of full size, to fit the gallery, the module was equipped to let visitors perform simulated space experiments, use a closed-circuit camera to work an exterior robotic arm, or try on a sleep restraint that astronauts use to keep from floating around the cabin. They could even peer into a space toilet.

The museum wanted the exhibit to create a sense of exploration and to be highly interactive. One of the ways the project team met these goals was to have teams of 12

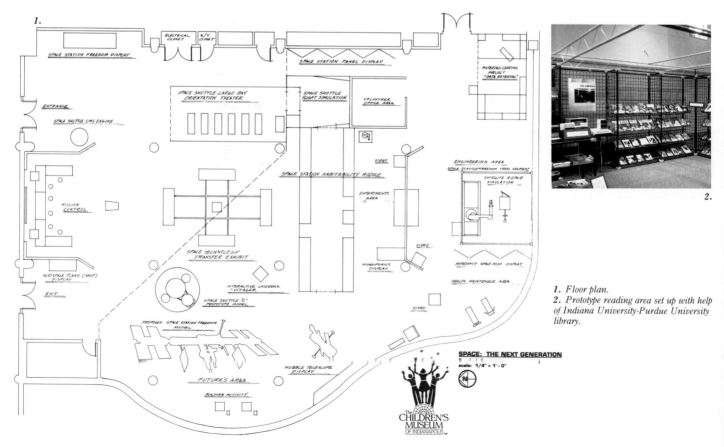

1. Floor plan.
2. Prototype reading area set up with help of Indiana University-Purdue University library.

children (picked by lottery) run simulated space shuttle flights. Six children sat in front of screens at mission control—set up against the wall between the gallery's two entrance doors. Six other children climbed to the shuttle's simulated flight deck. All wore NASA flight suits and wireless radio headsets. Briefed by the museum flight staff, the kids would then read from a script and throw switches in special sequences activating computer-controlled laser-disk programs. The "astronauts" would observe blast-off on video screens outside the cabin windows, actual NASA footage of launch, orbit, and landing seen from the flight commander's chair. In the control center, the ground crew and visitors observed the "astronauts" on closed-circuit TV and could follow the flight on

3.

4.   5.

3. Overhead are flags of countries that signed the Space Station Agreement and an actual segment of the Space Station Freedom's supporting truss.
4. Mock-up of Space Station Freedom's Habitability Module.
5. Tables hold model-building toys so children can design future space vehicles.

6.

a large central screen. The missions lasted half an hour.

The museum team borrowed a considerable amount of space hardware. From the Marshall Space Flight Center in Huntsville came a replica of the Hubble space telescope built to a scale of about 1 to 15, and a 20'-long model of the space station Freedom, which Steven Sipe suspended on aircraft cable from the Unistrut system embedded in the gallery's ceiling. Also from Marshall came a 15'-tall model of the proposed space shuttle C, an unmanned cargo vessel. At the

far end of the gallery was an industrial arm like the one used on the shuttle but smaller, loaned by its manufacturer, GMF Robotics. Using a computer keyboard, visitors could instruct the arm to change a space-satellite battery.

Sipe learned what it was like to sit in a flight chair and got an idea of scale from his visits to NASA installations. He designed a simulated flight deck console, fabricated from plywood with a laminate covering, inset with lights, switches, and simulated instruments.

From NASA's Langley Research Center in Virginia came a full-scale segment of the supporting truss of the space station Freedom. Sipe suspended that, too, from the ceiling just above the space station model. Also displayed was an orbital maneuvering

system (OMS) just like one of the two fitted to the rear of each space shuttle.

The exhibit's colors were primarily those used by NASA—grays, red, yellow, black, and white. But overhead, Sipe suspended 4'-by-8' flags of the countries that have signed the Space Station Agreement; these lent more color to the exhibit, along with the color transparencies in the windows.

But there were still more things for visitors to do. They could go to a health station and do exercises prescribed for the astronauts in space or monitor their blood pressure. In a comfortable, carpeted 350-sq.-ft. area, they could look at or borrow books or videotapes displayed on black wire racks in a prototype program set up between the museum and the Indiana University-Purdue University library. Borrowed

material could be returned at any public library in Indiana. In an area called "Beyond Tomorrow," in the space cupped by the gallery's curved wall, Sipe set up two tables and put out a model-building toy so that children could dream up future space vehicles.

Along the gallery walls, Sipe installed several panel displays supplied by NASA: one of a Hubble telescope from the Marshall Space Flight Center; one of a space station; and a foods-in-space display from Houston.

At various times during the exhibit's 2-month stay, astronauts and space engineers came to give scheduled talks, and twice the gallery provided live coverage of a space launch from Cape Canaveral.

In all, Sipe says, the exhibition was much richer than he'd envisioned. This may have

7.

8.

been due partly to the way the large-scale space machines filled the space and partly to the response to the simulated space missions, when 40 or 50 persons might be standing around "mission control," observing.

Sipe says he enjoyed working with people from so many different backgrounds, but he was particularly "thrilled" by the excitement of the children. "You should have seen the faces of the kids who went on a 'space mission,'" he exults. Sipe reports that he got calls afterward from teachers telling him how the exhibit had motivated children to be more attentive to news about space, and more willing to do research on it. On busy days, the exhibit drew as many as 5000 visitors.

The Children's Museum put the exhibit together in a year on a budget of $120,000.

9.

10.

6. Shoulder patch has exhibit's logo.
7, 10. Exhibit visitors fly a simulated mission from mock-up of space shuttle flight deck.
8. Inside mock-up of Space Station Freedom's Habitability Module.

9. Rendering exhibit entrance.
11. Rendering of robotic arm like that in space shuttle's engineering bay.

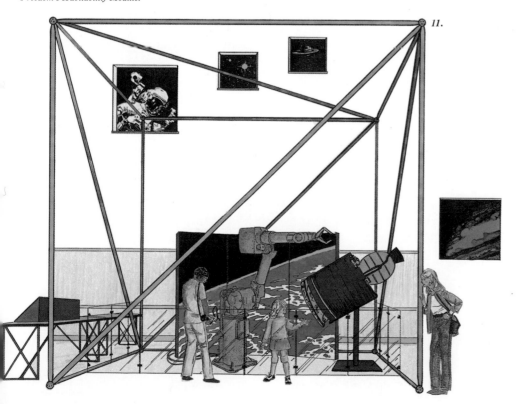

11.

Client: The Children's Museum (Indianapolis, IN)
Sponsors: Eli Lilly and Co., Lilly Endowment, NASA Lewis Research Center, W.K. Kellogg Foundation, GMF Robotics Corp., Allison Transmission Div./World Transmission Team, Delco Remy Div. GMF
Design firm: The Children's Museum
Designers: Steven W. Sipe (exhibit), Sheila Jackson (logo)
Consultants: Mark Horn, Educational Resources, NASA Lewis Research Center; NASA Lyndon B. Johnson Space Center; NASA George C. Marshall Space Flight Center; Rick Crosslin, Robert S. Foerster (aerospace educators); ARAC
Fabricators: The Children's Museum; NASA; The Exhibit House, Inc.; Thorp Awnings; Hellar Co.

Constructing Light:
Minimal Lighting Design 1900-1988

Susan Bower and Stephen Leet of Bower Leet Architects found themselves in the unusual position of being their own clients for this exhibit of 20th-century minimalist light fixtures. Bower, at the time, was an adjunct professor at the Parsons School of Design in New York City, and the school had asked its faculty for exhibit suggestions. Bower, who had become fascinated with lamps and lighting while designing interiors after graduating from architectural school, convinced the school of the virtues of minimalist lighting fixtures as an exhibit. The way she envisioned it, the fixtures would make a design statement, and so would the exhibit lighting, which would come entirely from the fixtures displayed. And that is what happened.

Bower and Leet did everything themselves. As fundraisers, they raised $7500 to provide the budget. As researchers and curators, they decided which lamps to display, then went out and found actual examples. As designers, they designed the exhibit. As their own clients, they approved the final design. And, as fabricators, they put together and installed the display cases, backdrops, and wiring.

Measuring 70′ by 30′ by 17′ high, the space could have swallowed the 36 minimalist fixtures, the largest of which stood only a spindly 6′ tall, the shortest 6″. They solved this problem by designing open-faced wooden cases to isolate each lamp. Constructed of unfinished birch plywood, each case stood 7′ high, 3′ wide, and 2′ deep. To reflect the light, Bower and Leet lined the

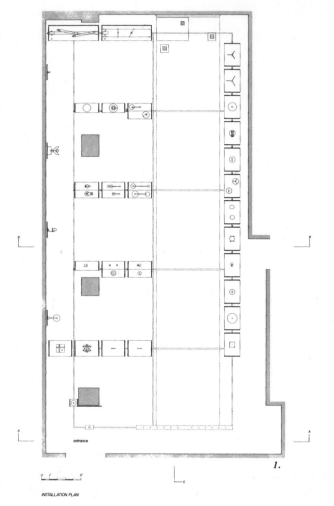

1. Installation plan.
2, 3. Elevation drawings of two exhibit rows.
4. Each lighting fixture has its own birch case. Table lamps sit on shelf at case's midpoint.
5. All the exhibit's lighting comes from the lamps displayed. On front wall, Miranda and King's Channel 1 System illuminates photos of lamps the designers couldn't include in exhibit.

INSTALLATION PLAN

1.

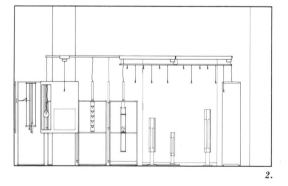

2.

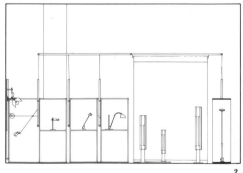

3.

interior back panel of each case with white drafting vellum. Reaching 3′ above the top of each case, and running down its side, was a gray-painted galvanized steel conduit to guide wires from the gallery's overhead lighting track into each case. Supplying power to each lamp without creating a snakes's nest of wires on the gallery floor had been their biggest initial concern.

To save money, yet be able to see that case dimensions and sight lines were accurate in the initial design, they built no prototypes or models; they merely taped the dimensions of display boxes to the studio walls.

These cases, however, did more than just house lamps and reflect light. Lined up 4″ apart against one wall, 12 of the cases began to fill the space in a way the individual lamps could never do. Then, three rows of three cases each and one row of four cases were placed perpendicularly to the row of 12, across an open space left as an aisle. These further filled the gallery, providing the bulk and uniformity needed to give the exhibit definition. Each case in three of these perpendicular rows was divided into two back-to-back cases of two compartments each by a vertical plywood panel running down the middle and a horizontal shelf at a height of 3½′. In these cases, the designers placed a small table lamp on each shelf.

The first of the perpendicular rows had floor lamps in see-through cases which had no backing. This row, near the entrance, let visitors see into the exhibit. On a structural

4.

5.

6.

column just inside the entrance, the designers placed a text panel explaining the show. Next to this column, in a narrow (6″-wide) see-through case, stood one of Achille Castiglioni's Bulb Lamps as a sort of logotype for the show.

Just to the right of the entrance on the end wall, Bower and Leet mounted photo blowups of lamps they couldn't obtain. To light these blowups, the designers suspended a plywood soffit from the gallery's lighting grid, and from the soffit they hung a dozen halogen lamps, the Channel 1 System by Miranda and King.

From this front wall, the aisle formed by the light cases stretched 70′ to the rear of the gallery. To help define that aisle, the designers ran a canopy of gray photo paper overhead behind the ceiling

lighting grid and then allowed the roll of paper to drop to the floor at the end of the gallery. There, against the photo paper on the rear wall, they placed a family of three fluorescent fixtures, designed in 1959-60 by Sergve Mouille, which he calls "Signals." (Mouille named the tallest, which is about 6′, "Le Gran Signal," and the shortest, 3′, "Le Petit Signal"). The photo paper also provided an overhead surface that reflected the lighting, helping give the entire gallery space a soft glow.

Bower and Leet took a leisurely and sporadic year-and-a-half to research the exhibit, then constructed and installed it in a week.

The Casebook jurors called it refreshing.

8.

6. *View toward front of gallery.*
7. *View toward back of gallery. Wiring for each lamp comes from ceiling grid through steel conduit into top of each case.*
8. *Vertical plywood panels in some of the birch cases convert them into back-to-back cases.*

Sponsoring institution: Parsons School of Design Exhibition Center (New York, NY), Clinton Kuopus, director
Sponsors: New York State Council on the Arts; New School for Social Research Faculty Development Fund
Design firm: Bower Leet Architects, St. Louis, MO
Designers: Susan Bower, Stephen Leet; Patricia Phillips, Marta Gutman, Linda Levy (special assistance)
Fabricator: Chris Lehrecke (cabinetmaker)

Geological Architecture:
The Work of Stanley Saitowitz

Like the other six architects who participated in the Walker Art Center's Architecture Tomorrow series, Stanley Saitowitz was asked to create a space that would convey his architectural philosophy. Saitowitz, who teaches at the University of California/ Berkeley, and runs his own San Francisco office, Stanley Saitowitz Architects, sees architecture as "space modulated with matter," and as "the construction of situations—ambiences qualitatively transformed."

At the Walker, Saitowitz transformed a 2000-sq.-ft. gallery and part of a roof terrace by creating an architectural structure that did two functional things: It served as a display device for models of his architecture and provided ways of viewing them from different perspectives. Concrete supports about 3' high, shaped sometimes a little like vertical I-beams and sometimes like thin wafers, held glass runways or shelves about 1' wide and as long as 18' to 20'. Three of these lined up parallel to one another, divided only by a wooden ramp and a metal catwalk or bridge, served as display surfaces for models (⅛" to 1') of Saitowitz's work. Along both ramp and bridge were other vertical elements— gray-painted steel and plywood sandwich panels. The ramp, bridge, and final stairs that led visitors down to the unpainted particle-board-covered gallery floor channeled their forward movement, allowing them what Saitowitz calls "spatial involvement." As they moved along Saitowitz's pathways, they could view the models

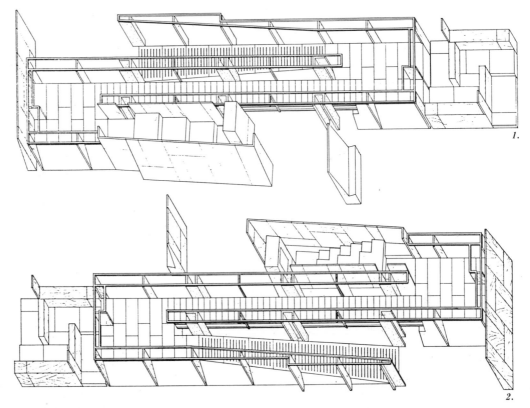

1.

2.

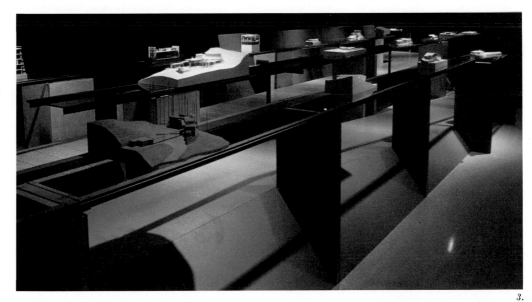

3.

1, 2. Isometric drawing of architect Stanley Saitowitz's exhibit framework seen with entrance at top (Fig. 1) and entrance at bottom (Fig. 2).
3. Saitowitz's geological-architectural framework with models of his work in place.

4.

from above, from below, and from various sides.

Saitowitz's structure, composed of elements that might be used in a building, is a work of architecture in itself. And more than providing display surfaces and offering guidance in moving past and viewing the displays, it filled the gallery's anonymous space. It became a space within a space. In light of Saitowitz's philosophy, it became "geology," growing from what he called the "horizon" of the particle-board covering of the gallery floor. "Horizon is a metaphor for reaching for the sky," says Saitowitz, and that is what his structure did, though the sky may have been invisible beyond the gallery's 13′ ceiling. The structure also extended visually through the gallery's glass wall onto the roof terrace, where

Saitowitz had designed low, box-like forms arranged like interlocking Ls and painted green in contrast to an unpainted particle-board base. These offered seats from which to view the Minneapolis skyline.

Saitowitz built models of his work especially for this exhibit, crafting them of redwood, walnut, mahogany, metal, and Styrofoam. He tried to bring out the differing qualities of the designs, some of which were still proposals, some in construction, and some, completed buildings. Lined up on the glass shelves, each of the 20 models had its plan silkscreened on the glass next to it. Overhead lights shone through the plans, outlining them on the gallery floor.

The glass shelves were intended to be more than just platforms. They became for

Saitowitz a "second horizon" out of which the models rose to "capture space." "Architecture is the purposeful demarcating of space," he says. "Architecture occurs at the junction of mind and site."

As visitors walked up the wooden ramp beside the models, they could see a downtown Minneapolis church steeple in their line of sight through the gallery's glass wall. They made a U-turn to walk along the metal bridge that led between two rows of models. Then they made another U-turn and went down a short flight of steps through what Saitowitz calls an amphitheater, where a videotape provided information about his architectural models.

The exhibit traveled to the Museum of Photography in Riverside, California, and to the San Francisco Museum of

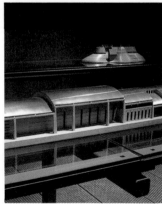

5.

Modern Art.

Saitowitz put the exhibition together in one year on a budget of $45,000.

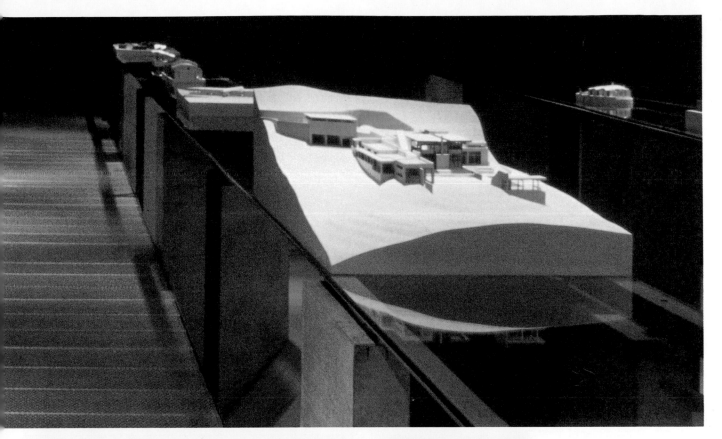

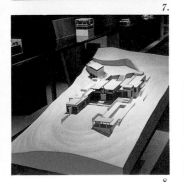

4, 5. *Models of Saitowitz's architecture rest on glass runways separated by walkways and ramps.*
6. *Concrete structural forms support both runways and walkways.*
7. *On stairs at end of exhibit, visitor watches a video explaining Saitowitz's work.*
8. *Model of Saitowitz's design for the Dinapoli residence in Los Gatos, CA.*

Client: Walker Art Center (Minneapolis, MN)
Sponsors: The Jay Chiat Foundation; Graham Foundation for Advanced Studies in the Fine Arts; Helen and Kim Whitney
Design firm: Stanley Saitowitz Architects, San Francisco, CA
Designer: Stanley Saitowitz

6.

7.

8.

Keith W. Johnson Zoo Center

The Zoo Center newly opened at New York City's Bronx Zoo was once the elephant house. A copper-domed Beaux Arts building, the Center stands just inside the zoo's west gate, surrounded by a clutter of other structures—a cafeteria, a children's zoo, a service area, the quarter-acre of formal gardens in front of the Center (with their newly sculpted bronze rhinoceroses) and the roadway that enters the west gate and snakes through the zoo. At first, zoo officials thought of moving the elephants elsewhere and using the building solely as the zoo's main information center. But the New York Zoological Society's general director, William Conway, decided that it was important to keep the elephants, and other great rare mammals, at the center of the zoo, where they would be a symbol of the Society's commitment to conservation.

This decision was factored in when the Society refurbished the fine 1908 Beaux Arts building originally designed by Heinz and LaFarge. They restored its roof, took out the old barred cages that lined the inner space of its wings, repointed its interior brickwork, and created between two and three acres of trees, grass, shrubs, and ponds around the building in what had been asphalt-covered spaces. In these natural habitats, carefully removed from zoo visitors by invisible barriers, are two elephants, an older female and a young male, two tapirs and one Sumatran rhinoceros, a female, one of only 400 still surviving. In an effort to save the species, the zoo hopes eventually to get

a male Sumatran rhino and have the two mate.

In creating an outdoor habitat reminiscent of a subtropical Asian monsoon forest, the zoo transplanted some 20,000 large-leafed trees, shrubs, and plants, representing more than 152 species. Volunteers planted 42,000 plugs of grass in the elephant area. To give the grass a chance of surviving under the pounding of elephant feet, the designers used specimens of eight particularly hardy grass species. They also layered the ground beneath the grass. The lowest layer is large gravel that shifts under pressure. This is topped by smaller, angular gravel, and a finer surface layer of a sand-soil mix.

Elephants are hard on all vegetation, not just grass. They eat young trees and shrubs, of course, but in just walking around they knock things down. Young elephants will even wrap their trunks around a tree or a bush and pull it up as a sort of play or test of strength. To preserve the habitat, the designers separated the wildlife from the edible vegetation with moats (and occasionally by very low-voltage cables) and hid the moats from visitors by using vegetation (sometimes man-made) and by controlling the position of viewing platforms. At one point, a fallen tree made of steel, fiberglass, and epoxy keeps animals from wandering down a dry stream bed to the public path. Logs of concrete and epoxy blended with natural brush hide the cable barriers that work, along with the moats, to keep the animals in the habitat.

Where possible, the

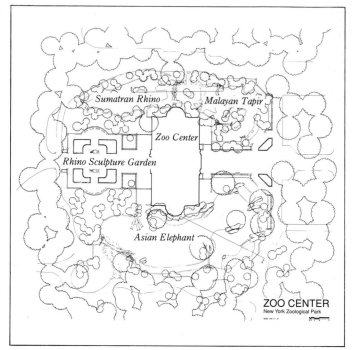

Sumatran Rhino   *Malayan Tapir*
Zoo Center
Rhino Sculpture Garden
Asian Elephant

ZOO CENTER
New York Zoological Park

1.

2.

1. Zoo Center site plan.
2. Renovated elephant house is now the Bronx Zoo's Zoo Center, housing elephants, tapirs, and rhinoceroses. Sculpted rhinos flank path to entrance.
3. Brass-edged light box in Center's central rotunda.
4. Surrounded by purple arches, light boxes and photo panels offer information on the Center's animals.
5. Sketch of the Center's two elephants.
6. Detail of rhino information.
7. Exterior copper donor's plaque with a vertigris finish and gold-fill, acid-etched letters.

25/Exhibition Design

designers set up viewing areas so that visitors can see elephants, rhinos, and tapirs in green, leafy settings without the intrusion of moats or buildings. At the outer edges of these viewing stations are chest-high wooden railings supported on painted steel rods. Just beyond the railings are 16″-by-44″ porcelain graphic panels, each on two 2″-diameter bronze legs which bend away from the viewer at 45 degrees to hold the panels. "We gave the bronze support legs a verdigris finish to blend with the copper roof of the building," says Charles H. Beier, associate director of EGAD, the New York Zoological Society's Exhibition and Graphic Arts Department.

Because the panels use a special 4-color process that bakes each color separately into the porcelain enamel, the designers could specify print and photographs that, according to Beier, come out with "an excellent quality almost like continuous line" and, of course, are protected from the outdoor environment. In the outdoor habitats, the panels use photos, sketches, and text to tell about the animals' anatomy and behavior. Text titles are set in Times Roman bold, "because of its classicism," says John Gwynne, New York Zoological Society deputy director for design. Body text is Helvetica light.

The site's three ponds are all close to a viewing platform. Each pond has a steep drop-off in the middle, so the animals can get into deeper water from the shore but can't climb out over hidden barriers into a very shallow, 6″-deep, area that

comes right up to the viewing platforms. This solution made it possible for viewers to stand within 5′ of rhinos and tapirs and slightly farther away, 15′, from the elephants, beyond the reach of their trunks.

Inside the old building, glass curtain walls now separate the two wings from the central rotunda. Concrete floors, divided by a dry moat, run the length of each wing where the old steel-barred cages were removed. On one side of the moat is an area for visitors, and on the other side, backed by wood-covered walls, is the living space of the animals, elephants in one wing and tapirs and rhinos in the other. Special heating, ventilating, and air-conditioning ducts at the backs of the animal areas suck the air out and replenish it so that animal odors do not linger in the building.

Just in front of the walls opposite the animals are what amount to giant lightboxes behind 12′-high purple wooden arches. These arches rise from wooden capitals, designed and painted to mirror the building's original limestone capitals. The designers chose the Postmodern arches to break with the Beaux Arts architecture, to give a contemporary look to the design of a graphics device that deals with contemporary issues.

Yet the capitals and the purple color, which is really a medley of orange, green, and purple paint spots, are meant to give the arches a familial tie with the richly colored old brickwork behind them. "The arches were meant to embellish the architecture," says Beier, "but not to look built in."

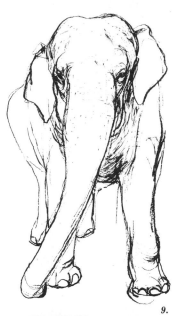

9.

The glass-fronted display devices (lighted by fluorescent tubes) hold graphics, shadow boxes with small animal models, and backlit transparencies meant to explain the great mammals and to bolster the zoo's conservation efforts. Some of the photos show the carcasses of elephants killed for their ivory tusks and rhinos killed for their horns, and the images are meant to be unsettling. But some of the photos are beautiful—a herd of elephants moving across dry savannah and a close-up of a rhino's skin.

10.

11.

In the rotunda's center sits a hexagonal desk, designed specially to come apart and be moved into a corner during special events. Then it is used to dispense drinks instead of brochures and memberships.

The Casebook jurors praised the way the Zoo Center's natural habitat suits both the animals and the old building it surrounds. But they called the purple arches in the interior "weak."

8. *Elephants and tapirs (inset) in Zoo Center's natural settings.*
9. *Elephant sketch.*
10, 11. *Porcelain enamel graphic panels on bronze legs offer information on animal anatomy and behavior.*

Client: New York Zoological Society (Bronx, NY), William Conway (general director), James Doherty (general curator)
Sponsors: City of New York and private donors
Design firms: New York Zoological Society Exhibition and Graphic Arts Department; Goldstone and Hinz; Coe, Lee, Robinson, Roesch; Joseph A. Wetzel Associates, Inc.
Designers: William Conway, James Doherty, John Gwynne, Charles H. Beier, Mark Wourms, Lee Ehmke, Meredith Zafonte, Chris Maune (supervisor, graphic production), Gary Smith (supervisor, exhibit production), Hank Tusinski (artist-in-residence), Jill Cowen (artifact researcher), Theodore Hinz, Jon Coe, Peter Alusitz, Joseph Wetzel, Tevere McFadyen, Mary McCloughlin (project coordinator, graphic design), George Bird, Pam Amster (photo research)
Fabricators: Cemrock Landscapes (Tucson, AZ), Production House (Ashburn, VA), New York Zoological Society's Exhibition and Graphic Arts Dept., Deborah Ross, Katherine Weems (bronze rhinoceros sculptor), U. S. Fish & Wildlife Service Region 5

8.

Tech 2000 Gallery

The clients envisioned the Tech 2000 Gallery as a place where people could try out the latest interactive video devices. They wanted it to provide spaces for manufacturers to set up and show off their latest interactive machines and programs, in an atmosphere that would encourage visitors to settle in, to touch—to interact with—the equipment. The Gallery would take up 10,000 sq. ft. in Washington, DC's Techworld Plaza.

The clients were Tech 2000, Inc., and the trade group IMA (Interactive Multimedia Association). After asking several exhibit designers to come up with concepts for the space, they selected a concept by Edwin Schlossberg, Inc., of New York City and asked Schlossberg to design the Gallery. Included was to be a special orientation area, presenting interactive video in a historical perspective.

The client wanted the space organized around six themes: arts and culture, working, learning, the home, public services, and computer/video simulations.

Before being selected to do the design, Schlossberg had been involved in helping the client decide on the Gallery's physical requirements. They decided they wanted an environment flexible enough to be unaffected by continually changing video programs and equipment.

The designers used color, light, and partitions both to unify and to divide the space (which was punctuated at 20' intervals by concrete support columns). About the partitions, they were particular. They

wanted a partition system that would give both privacy and a sense of openness. They wanted it to look elegant, warm, and a little high-tech—but not too much. The partitions they designed are about 8' high, vary in width from 4' to 6', and are 6" thick. Screws hold two metal sheets, perforated in a regular pattern, to either side and to either end of a wooden frame that has a natural finish with a slight sheen. These panels were attached to the Gallery's concrete columns, to the floor and occasionally, where there were two columns, to the ceiling. Some light comes through the perforations.

Color, carried throughout the Gallery beneath a gray ceiling and a black ceiling grid, is teal-green and deep blue on the walls and gray in the carpet.

Perhaps the most important unifying element, though, is an arrangement of full-size mannequins. The designers had 18 of these specially designed and positioned throughout the space in poses that indicate, the way department store mannequins do with clothes, how visitors might use the equipment. Designed with stock mannequin bodies, given heads and hands modeled from real persons, and clothed to suit the situations they illustrate, the mannequins invite visitors to use the equipment, to settle in and sample the various programs.

Visitors enter past one of these mannequins peering up through his spectacles at a sphere of information in the entranceway. Actually, this sphere is just a slice, a one-quarter sphere placed against

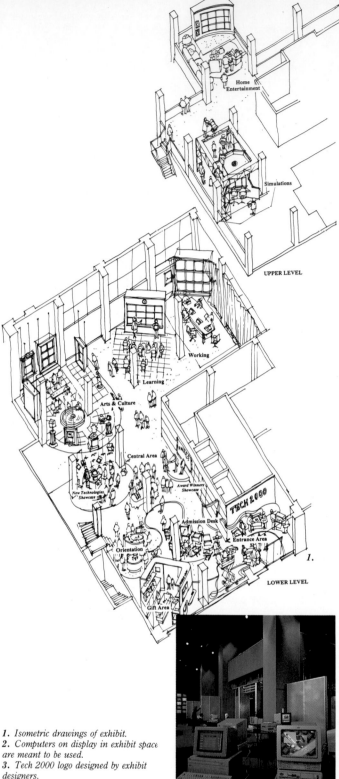

1. Isometric drawings of exhibit.
2. Computers on display in exhibit space are meant to be used.
3. Tech 2000 logo designed by exhibit designers.
4, 5. Mannequins are meant to invite visitors to use equipment being exhibited.

2.

an angle of mirrors. On it are letters cut from foam spelling out areas of knowledge, such as biology, sociology, etc.

In the reception area inside, a woman mannequin is holding a smaller sphere of information. Overhead is a three-tiered circular soffit 20′ in diameter, which has a coat of frosted paint. In one corner is a reception desk made of wood panels and trimmed in black metal and Formica.

Beyond the desk, the bright lights of the Communication Day Parade draw visitors toward it. This colorful scale-model diorama celebrates the history of communications and is the device used by the Schlossberg designers to put interactive video in its historical place. Here is a parade of some 2000 plaster-sculpted human figures 3″ or 4″ tall (some are modified off-the-shelf model-railroad and doll-house figures). Most, 1500 or so, are painted a uniform gray and stand on the sidelines watching the parade. The remaining figures, painted with gaily colored clothes, take part in the parade's floats. Floats and figures parade in a 20′-long glass case, atop a black Formica-covered plywood base, waist-high and lighted from a 6″ soffit on the case's top. Each float has a human-communications theme, from speech, to book printing and radio, to computers and satellites.

Text panels about 6″ square explain these communications briefly. Designers tilted the panels toward the viewer by propping their inner edges on miniature saw horses, patterned after the kind used to keep back crowds at parades.

3.

4.

5.

The parade is fun, done in a humorous way, and Celia Pearce, the Schlossberg designer who served as project manager, gives a lot of credit to its fabricators. "It was done," she says, "by sculptors who do clay-animation and scale-model work for television. They breathed life into the parade. From the outset, they understood its intent and embellished it with their own details."

But beyond the parade's humor and history, it carries a subtle message. Its hundreds of tiny figures emphasize people, not machines. "It shows," says Celia Pearce, "people interacting with people *through* machines."

The rest of the exhibit space is designed to show off that technology in a way that

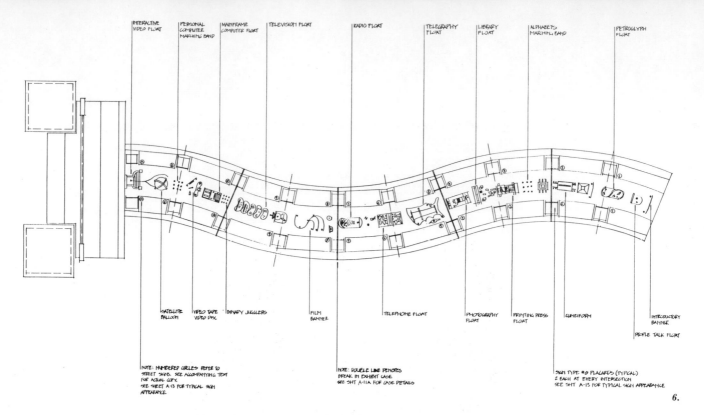

INTERACTIVE VIDEO FLOAT   PERSONAL COMPUTER MARCHING BAND   MAINFRAME COMPUTER FLOAT   TELEVISION FLOAT   RADIO FLOAT   TELEGRAPHY FLOAT   LIBRARY FLOAT   ALPHABETS MARCHING BAND   PETROGLYPH FLOAT

SATELLITE BALLOON   VIDEO TAPE VIDEO DISC   BINARY JUGGLERS   FILM BANNER   TELEPHONE FLOAT   PHOTOGRAPHY FLOAT   PRINTING PRESS FLOAT   CUNEIFORM   INTRODUCTORY BANNER   PEOPLE TALK FLOAT

NOTE: NUMBERED CIRCLES REFER TO STREET SIGNS. SEE ACCOMPANYING TEXT FOR ACTUAL COPY. SEE SHEET A-13 FOR TYPICAL SIGN APPEARANCE.

NOTE: DOUBLE LINE DENOTES BREAK IN EXHIBIT CASE SEE SHT A-11A FOR CASE DETAILS

SIGN TYPE #0 PLACARDS (TYPICAL) 2 EACH AT EVERY INTERSECTION SEE SHT A-13 FOR TYPICAL SIGN APPEARANCE

6.

encourages people to interact with it.

From the parade, visitors move into the arts and culture area. In a room created and divided by the perforated sheet-metal partitions, video screens (mounted on fluted pedestals) and wall-mounted monitors play the sort of interactive videos that might be used by art museums. One screen, for example, has information on a Picasso painting, and visitors use the keyboard to call up the particular information they want. A plaster mannequin of an art student stands sketching in front of one screen and its attendant slave monitor, which is wall-mounted in an ornate picture frame. Each pedestal is 3′6″ high by 1′10″ wide and houses a small computer and a fan which circulates air through vertical perforated metal strips running up the wooden fluting. Cords connect the computer to floor outlets through holes in the back of the pedestals.

Next is a transition area in which some current-model, big-screen TVs play. From here, visitors can either go straight ahead into the working area to view business uses of interactive machines or, to their left, go up stairs to see the way the machines can be used in the home.

On the stairs is a plaster mannequin of a well-dressed man carrying a bag of groceries, while, above him, his wife looks over a railing from her living room. At the top of the stairs are three rooms: a living room with cabinets holding equipment such as high-definition TV, home computers, and video disk players with lots of controls, where a plastic mannequin of the married couple's son is watching TV; a children's room furnished with custom-made furniture in primary colors, including an entertainment console; and an open area with naturally lacquered plywood walls where

Tech 2000 can set up large simulation equipment, such as a flight simulator.

Back on the main level, the working area has a conference table and individual work stations with modular school desks where visitors can test equipment. Full-sized mannequins man the phones.

In the education area are more school desks, lined up as if in a classroom, and a mannequin teacher in front of them is calling on a student mannequin in the back row who has her hand raised. All the desks have video screens and keyboards.

From the education area, visitors can circle back into an area the designers named the Town Center, a space defined by a 20′ triple-tiered circular soffit identical to that in the reception area. Ringing the Town Center are kiosks that display public interactive devices like banking machines and drug information and travel

information machines.

Throughout the Gallery, the lighting level is kept low. This allows the flickering light of the video screens to stand out, becoming a design element. Combined with the materials and the teal, blue, and gray colors, the lighting helps achieve an overall look that the designers feel is comfortable and inviting and, at the same time, says Celia Pearce, "slick, even futuristic."

Each area is designated by a pennant-shaped, glowing-edged sign about 6″ high and 3′ long fastened to a lightbox that spells out the area's purpose. At the entrance, the designers wall-mounted the logo they designed for the Tech 2000 Gallery, cutting the custom letters from foam and painting them black with red under-and-over lines.

The Schlossberg designers completed the project in six months on a budget of $440,000, which included $260,000 for fabrication.

7.

8.

9.

10.

6-10. *Communication Day Parade with 3" figures illustrates turning points in the history of communication.*

Client: Tech 2000, Inc.; Interactive Multimedia Association (Washington, DC); Techworld Trade Association
Sponsors: Major sponsors include Sony Corp., IBM, Apple Computer, Pioneer Communications, and more than 80 multimedia software developers. A list of sponsors can be obtained from Tech 2000.
Design firm: Edwin Schlossberg, Inc. (New York, NY)
Designers (primary team): Edwin Schlossberg (principal designer), Celia Pearce (project manager), Diane Klein (production manager), Marian Jamieson (senior project designer), Andrew Proehl (project designer), Lisa Strong (junior project designer)
Designers (secondary team): Bara Levin (content manager), Calasha Gish (writer), Dennis Cohen, Michael Joyce (initial concept design), David Bixby, Tim Burnham (technical consultation), Derek Conde, Peter Burns (drafting)
Consultants: Jeff Heger (exhibit photography), Andrew Proehl (additional photography), Andrew Proehl, Marian Jamieson (art direction on photography), Lisa Strong (coordination photography)
Fabricators: Acadia Scenic (David Lawson, president); Studio E.I.S. (Elliot Schwartz, Ivan Schwartz, principals)

We Were Children Just Like You

The Center for Holocaust Studies in Brooklyn, New York, gave Erik Schurink some 200 photographs of Jewish children taken at three distinct times: before, during, and after the Holocaust. They asked him to design a traveling exhibit using the photos (and accompanying personal histories) that would document the lives of these children. The first two installations, they told him, would be in Manhattan's 92nd Street YMHA and in Brooklyn's Borough Hall, and each would have approximately 1400 sq. ft. of exhibit space.

Schurink knew he had to devise a way of organizing the photos and text within the three time periods. He decided to mount the photos in groups of four on the surface of Masonite hollow-core doors. These doors were thereafter treated as display panels and were grouped according to the dates of the photos on them.

The designer knew, too, that people would spend more time reading if he kept the text short, so he pared it down to three or four lines beneath each photo. Next, he statted the text on enlarged photostats, which he glued to Masonite photo-panels measuring 2' by 2½'. Then, he spot-mounted every panel's four photos, each above its appropriate caption, and enclosed the photo-panels in narrow walnut frames that were later painted. Wooden cleats screwed to the back of each photo-panel hooked over cleats on the lightweight door-panels.

During the design process, Schurink realized that, despite the subject matter, black-and-

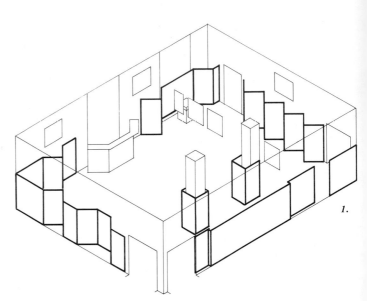

1.

2.

white photos mounted on Masonite doors don't make a very arresting exhibit, and he began thinking of the door-panels as surfaces for murals. These murals, he reasoned, would become a backdrop for the photos, setting a mood and helping establish context with color and graphic images. By fastening from one or two up to eight or nine door-panels together with angled brackets, Schurink created surfaces as wide as 27' for each mural. He made brackets available in three angles—90 degrees, 135 degrees, and 180 degrees—so these panels could be fastened together at the various installations in configurations angled to suit the sites.

Schurink wanted a mural for each of the exhibit's three time periods—pre-Holocaust,

3.

1. Isometric drawing of installed exhibit.
2, 3. Hollow core door panels hold photos in groups of four. Murals relating to the exhibit's three time periods tie the door panels in each section together.

Holocaust, and post-Holocaust—and he sought a different artist for each. "I selected three mural artists with distinctly different styles," he says, "to ensure that each time period retained its own identity." He gave them specific instructions: He wanted the murals to be "faded and expressionistic" so they wouldn't clash with the photographs. And he gave them reference materials—photos, sketches, and descriptions of the time periods.

Working closely with Schurink, each artist came up with a mural that evoked the mood of the era. For instance, the artist for the prewar era had a style that played with light, soft colors, and textures, symbolizing, Schurink notes, "a time of freedom and no hardships." The client

suggested a mural filled with fields of buttercups and that (nine panels), along with images of the Hebrew alphabet and a synagogue (one panel), is what the artist produced.

The dark somber colors of the war-era mural reflect "oppression and death," and its images are stormy seas (four panels), the ghetto wall (four panels), railroad tracks (two panels), woods and bushes (two panels), and a hiding place (two panels).

A horizon, with a sunny blue sky and green shoots sprouting from a barren landscape, is the mural for the postwar era (eight panels). The photographs show children being liberated and trying to find lost family and friends.

Throughout the exhibit, the photos are mostly posed shots of children in groups—sports,

school, church, family, and concentration camp groups.

In the war area, the photostats behind the photos are black with white Times Roman type; in the pre- and postwar areas, the photostats are white with black Times Roman. Schurink painted the frames of each photo-panel to blend with the mural behind it.

Schurink put the exhibit together in 4 months on a budget of $38,000. It was to travel to five or six museums in Europe before coming to rest as a permanent exhibit at Kibbutz Lohamei Haghettaot in Israel, a kibbutz museum which is building a special pavilion, a wing on the existing museum, to house it.

4.

4, 5. Photos mounted on Masonite, black for the war years, with narrow walnut frames.
6. Mural detail of ghetto wall.

6.

Client: Center for Holocaust Studies (Brooklyn, NY), Yaffa Eliach, executive director
Sponsors: New York State Department of Education; Brooklyn delegation of the New York State Legislature; Federal Republic of Germany; plus donations of private foundations and individuals (a list is available from the Center for Holocaust Studies)
Design firm: E Design, New York, NY
Designer: Erik Schurink
Scenic painters: Sally Johnnes (prewar era), Carol May (war era), Elizabeth Sadoff (postwar era)
Fabricators: Tim Watkins; Superior

Photos by Scott Dorance

5.

Minneapolis Sculpture Garden

The Minneapolis Sculpture Garden is the Walker Art Center's 7½-acre outdoor sculpture gallery. Designed by Edward Larrabee Barnes, architect of the Walker's present building, in association with landscape architect Peter Rothschild of Quennell Rothschild Associates, the Garden consists of four 100-sq.-ft. plazas planted with Kentucky bluegrass, divided by a cruciform walkway lined with linden trees. Evergreens (arborvitae) in low granite planters define each plaza. The museum uses the two southernmost plazas, those closest to the Walker-Guthrie Theater complex, for temporary exhibitions. The two north plazas hold works from the Walker's permanent collection, scuptures by Ellsworth Kelly, Mark di Suvero, Richard Serra, and Tony Smith.

Under the lindens along the walkway are works by such sculptors as Noguchi, Moore, Marini, Butterfield, and Lipchitz. Beneath the pyramid roof of the center house of the Sage and John Cowles Conservatory, the three graceful contiguous glass houses that Edward Larrabee Barnes designed to stand at the Sculpture Garden's west side, is Frank Gehry's sculpture "Standing Glass Fish," flipping above a palm-fringed lily pond.

Some of the Garden's 40 sculptures are part of the exhibit design. For instance, behind the conservatory is "Belvedere," a cedar sculpture by Jackie Ferrara meant to be a seating area and viewing platform as well as a work of art. In front of the conservatory

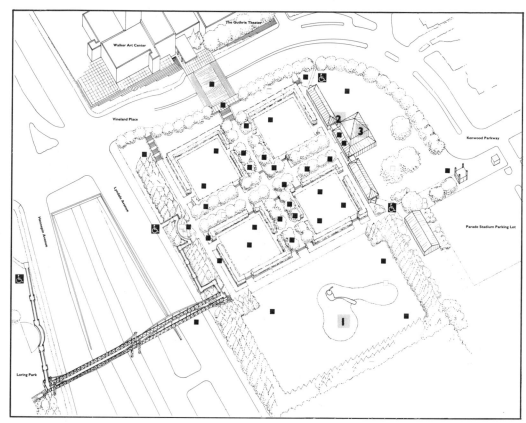

1. Spoonbridge and Cherry.
2. Regis Gardens, Cowles Conservatory.
3. Standing Glass Fish.

1.

2.   3.

1. Sculpture garden site plan.
2, 3. Sculpture garden's glass Conservatory, designed by Edward Larrabee Barnes, glows at night and shimmers by day in front of footbridge designed by Siah Armajani.

are benches of granite, basalt, and cedar by artist Kinji Akagawa, and along one of the walkways, benches of granite and cast iron by artist Philip Larson.

Visitors enter the Garden from the Walker down the striped granite walkway designed by minimalist artist Sol LeWitt. At the far end of the Garden, beyond the four plazas, is a rectangular grassy area about the size of a football field framed in Black Hills spruce. Resting in a pond in this field is a fountain sculpture of a bright red cherry resting in a white spoon (29′ high and 52′ long) by Coosje van Bruggen and her husband, Claes Oldenburg. Finally, crossing Interstate 94 to the east, linking the Sculpture Garden with Loring Park, part of the Minneapolis park system, is a graceful double-arched, pastel-colored footbridge, 375′ long, designed by artist Siah Armajani.

The Minneapolis Park and Recreation Board maintains and provides security for this largest urban sculpture garden in the nation.

4.

5.

6.

7.

4. *Frank Gehry's "Standing Glass Fish" inside the Conservatory.*
5. *Regis Gardens inside one of the Conservatory wings.*
6, 7. *Claes Oldenburg and Coosje van Bruggen's "Spoonbridge and Cherry" sculpture in Sculpture Garden's fountain pool.*

Client: Walker Art Center (Minneapolis, MN); Minneapolis Park and Recreation Board; Minnesota Landscape Arboretum, University of Minnesota
Funding donors: The McKnight Foundation; Sage and John Cowles; The Minneapolis Foundation/Irene Hixon Whitney Family Founder-Advisor Fund; Persephone Foundation; Wheelock Whitney; The Regis Foundation; The Bush Foundation; Lucy and Donald Dayton; The Kresge Foundation; Honeywell, Inc.; Cold Spring Granite Co. A list of additional donors and sponsors can be obtained from the Walker Art Center.
Construction support and services: U.S. Department of Transportation, Federal Highway Administration, Minnesota Department of Transportation, City of Minneapolis, National Endowment for the Arts
Designers: Edward Larrabee Barnes, New York, NY; Peter Rothschild, Quennell Rothschild Associates, New York, NY

Discovery Cove

The New York Aquarium calls its new marine education center Discovery Cove, and the first thing visitors see as they approach the building from the Coney Island boardwalk on the Atlantic Ocean, which it faces, is a lobster boat riding calmly in a man-made cove by the building's front entrance. Though the lobster boat is part of the exhibit, visitors don't get really close to it until they leave the building. But, as they enter over a wooden bridge that crosses the tiny artificial cove, they hear the voices of radio operators on New York Harbor's freighters and tugs talking on a taped loop, playing from a speaker in the lobster boat's cabin. Eventually, visitors will be able to go aboard and see how lobstermen haul traps and tell whether lobsters are big enough to keep.

Throughout Discovery Cove's exhibits, the designers used sound recorded in 3- or 4-minute segments on loops that play at seven positions in the building. "We purposely kept the volume low," says Richard Lyons of Lyons/Zaremba, Inc., the Boston design firm that provided project management for the exhibits' fabrication and installation and designed the graphics. "We wanted the sound to register subliminally, not take over. It is not the main event."

The main event—which starts almost immediately—consists of 70 individual aquatic exhibits that display as many as 1800 animals in 129,000 gallons of water.

Visitors pass a 3-photo mural, just inside the entrance, showing three natural aquatic habitats: a beach, a salt marsh, and a rocky shore pocked with tidal pools. These three backlit color-photo blowups are all 8' tall and set up so they seem to share a common horizon at the top. Together, they stretch 16' along a wall that slants into a corridor where visitors pass the first of the three habitats shown in the mural: a 43' section of sandy beach onto which a mechanically driven wave continuously curls. Behind this, a sound loop plays seashore sounds.

At the end of the corridor, the space opens onto the second habitat: an 875-sq.-ft. salt marsh. Tufts of salt marsh grass grow in a foot or two of water beneath a skylight. At the marsh's edge is an acrylic panel about 2' high, holding back the water. Through this, visitors can see what's going on within the marsh. The designers set graphics in place in a channel in the weathered wood rail that caps the acrylic panel. Just in front of the panel is a long ledge running most of the marsh's length, a few inches off the floor, onto which youngsters can step to see out over the marsh. The ledge, and a small deck it runs into in one corner, were made out of wood from a section of the Coney Island boardwalk that was being dismantled in front of the aquarium.

Though a small touch, this ledge is typical of the kind of thought and experience that went into Discovery Cove's exhibit design. The staff, which had spent thousands of hours watching aquarium visitors, thought of many ways that design could ease and enrich these visits, mostly by families ranging in age from toddlers to

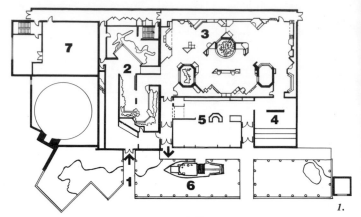

1. Entrance bridge.
2. Habitat exhibits.
3. Animal behavioral exhibits.
4. Changing exhibits.
5. Discovery Cove Village.
6. Discovery Cove Harbor.
7. Classrooms.

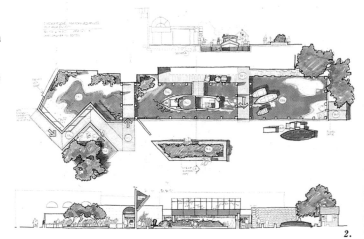

1. Floor plan.
2. Rendering of exhibits at Discovery Cove entrance.
3. Lobster boat in place at entrance.
4-8. Graphics cover aquarium walls, surrounding tanks. Note variety of tank configurations.

3.

4.

5.

6.

7.

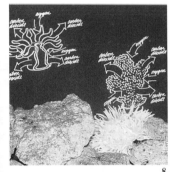

8.

grandparents. For example, brainstorming sessions that included the designers, museum staff, and fabricators, helped Charles Hruska, a staff preparator, to dream up seven mechanical devices to entertain children. He set these into the walls panels under the main exhibits, no more than a foot off the floor. Toddlers can do such things as push a button and see bubbles come out of a blowhole or turn a crank and hear the sound of a snapping shrimp that seems to come from the picture of one.

From the salt marsh, visitors make a sharp right turn and pass beneath an arched acrylic canopy. Through one side of the canopy they see a rocky shore and hear the sound of a distant foghorn. Overhead, waves break, the result of a 400-gallon bucket filling, tipping, and dumping its contents every 40 seconds. Water cascades down the canopy onto the rocks and trickles into tidal pools beyond the acrylic's protection. Here, docents and aquarium staff

allow visitors to touch tidal pool dwellers.

Just past the tidal pools is a wall covered with an 8′-high-by-16′ black-and-white mural of schooling fish. The fish seem to be swimming into the next exhibit room, leading the visitor on. The designers went out of their way to make the mural black and white, converting a color print. They meant the mural as a spot of repose, a pause. They wanted it to be background against which the color and excitement of the habitats and tanks would stand out.

The next room holds three large concrete tanks, each with from 12,000 to 14,000 gallons of water behind 10′- or 12′-high acrylic windows. Set up in a triangle in the 5640-sq.-ft. space, these tanks display a kelp bed, a coral reef, and a school of menhaden (an inedible, foot-long fish found near estuaries in the Atlantic and the Gulf of Mexico). On one side of the central coral reef is a grid ("a quilt," Dick Lyons calls it) of 1′-square color photos of the eyes of aquatic creatures. A tape loop plays bubbly and watery synthetic underwater sounds. Plenty of space for people to stand (or sit on a few built-in seats) exists between the tanks.

Around the periphery of the room, in alcoves built by extending wall panels into the space at intervals, are tanks and exhibits that explain how fish behave; how they eat, for instance, or swim, or reproduce. In the feeding area is a photo grid of animal mouths and teeth.

Discovery Cove, as the name implies, is meant to be a teaching facility. The teaching goes on informally through the explanatory texts silkscreened in Helvetica typeface (which the aquarium has always used) directly on the plastic laminate 9′ walls or on the acrylic tank windows. The designers also screened sketches on the dark blue walls using white ink containing a UV powder. This powder catches the light in a way that makes the drawings "evasive," says Lyons. "It makes them seem to float on the wall." Meant to illustrate and entertain, the sketches in the eating alcove show, for instance, the tooth-filled jaws of big fish chasing little fish. Graphic artist Sarah Landry did loose sketches on 8½″-by-11″ paper, then blew them up until a pencil line became an inch thick. Swirling along the panels around the wall tanks, the graphics unify the displays in each alcove.

Tanks come in all sizes and shapes. Sometimes, they project from the wall in elaborate profiles—a half barrel, maybe, or a ledge—meant to

enhance the impact of their inhabitants. Sometimes, they are recessed 9″ into the wall, leaving a ledge in front so that mothers, tired of lifting their toddlers up to see into the tank, can seat them on the ledge right against the tank's acrylic window. Metal rails 28″ off the floor stand in front of some tanks. These tubular rails, covered with plastic sleeves, are painted in colors meant to identify specific areas. Overhead, 10′ banners hang on aircraft cable from the ceiling. Their colors match those on the railings they hang above and their graphics mirror those on the wall.

To accommodate Discovery Cove's emphasis on teaching, the designers had small labs built in three locations behind the panels holding the large wall graphics. A teacher can open the wall panels and pull out racks with microscopes, video components, and artifacts. In two spaces around the coral reef tank, overhead doors (like garage doors) built into the ceiling come down to create rooms within a room where teachers who bring in groups of students can be sure of a captive audience.

Divers enter the three large tanks to clean the windows and feed the fish. Watching the divers work becomes part of the education.

To make the space in Discovery Cove's behavioral section as flexible as possible, the designers ran all plumbing and wiring under a floor made up of removable panels. If the aquarium wants to change tank placement and needs to reroute the plumbing and wiring, they lift out the appropriate panels

9.

10.

11.

9, 10. Graphic panels and habitats at aquarium entrance.
11. Tot pushes button to activate swim bladder device.

and reconfigure what's beneath.

Near the tank filled with the schooling menhaden is another photo grid of backlit animal photos. Each has a Microlouvre film over it, a film that screens the image from anyone looking at it from an angle greater than 45 degrees. As a result, the photogrid lights don't interfere with visibility in the schooling tank.

Just beyond the schooling tank, visitors leave the behavior room and move past a mini-theater, which has a large screen and built-in, carpet-covered step-seating. The space is meant for changing exhibits or use as a teaching area. When Discovery Cove first opened, a 3- to 4-minute video made by Lyons/Zaremba played on the mini-theater's screen. They went into New York City's parks and shot footage of the rich, natural environments, then ran it without narration, just picking up whatever sounds they encountered.

Right next to the mini-theater is a re-creation of a fishing village with several shops under a barrel-vaulted skylight: a ship's chandlery; fish, grocery, and apothecary stores, and a small gift shop. Only the gift shop is open for business. The others are just meant to evoke the flavor of a New England fishing village. In the background here, a tape loop plays what Lyons calls "the clack and clatter" of a fishing village—a lobster boat engine, a fog horn, boat repair work noise, and so on. But if the flavor is New England, the building materials originated in the South. The village's weathered boards came from a

decaying tobacco barn in Virginia. "We took the old boards, fireproofed them, smoked out the varmints, and used them for façades and window frames," Lyons says. Also in the village area is a central island, a cooking area where the staff can give cooking demonstrations.

The way out is past an 8'-high, 20'-long black-and-white mural of a real Maine fishing village. Once outside, visitors move along a wharf where the lobster boat is tied up in its artificial cove. Swimming in the cove (at least in good weather) are the aquarium's collection of turtles. The staff hopes they may eventually lay eggs in the cove's tiny beaches.

Design and construction of Discovery Cove took six years on an exhibit budget of $3.5 million.

13.

12.

12. Plexiglas canopy shields visitors from wave in habitat at exhibit entrance.
13-15. Shops in recreation of New England fishing village at exhibit's end.

14.

15.

Client: New York Zoological Society: New York Aquarium (Brooklyn, NY), Lewis Garibaldi, director
Sponsors: Achelis Foundation; Barker Welfare Foundation; Bodman Foundation; Charles A. Dana Foundation, Inc.; Cleveland H. Dodge Foundation, Inc.; Foundation for the Needs of Others, Inc.; Horace W. Goldsmith Foundation; Greenwall Foundation; Charles Hayden Foundation; Hillside Capital Incorporated; Atholl McBean Foundation; Dunlevy Milbank Foundation, Inc.; Howard Phipps Foundation; Mary and Laurance Rockefeller; Schiff Foundation; Iphigene Ochs Sulzberger; G. Unger Vetlesen Foundation; Women's Committee of the New York Zoological Society
Design firms: Jerry M. Johnson, Inc. (master planning and exhibit design); Lyons/Zaremba, Inc. (exhibit graphic design and exhibit project management), Richard Lyons, principal, Frank Zaremba, principal, Roger Carter, designer; Al Zanetti (village signs)
Architect: Ted Hines, Goldstone and Hines
Consultants: David L. Manwarren Corp. (habitat production); Sarah Landry (graphic mural artist); Monadnock Media (audiovisual production); Mary Jane Soule (sound artist); Ellie Fries, Merryl Kafka, Karen Hensel (New York Aquarium)
Fabricator: Exhibits Unlimited, Inc.

Whales, Giants of the Deep

What Daniel Quan wanted to design was an exhibit that took visitors beneath the surface of the sea to watch whales swimming in an atmosphere that would seem to earth dwellers like a somewhat blurred blue-green twilight. The atmosphere he wanted to create, and how he planned to establish it, were concepts difficult to communicate to his client, the Pacific Science Center in Seattle. He couldn't draw what he had in mind, so he made a model (¼" to 1'), lighted it with colored lights, added some sound, and produced a video.

Quan, of Daniel Quan Design in San Francisco, joined the project just as the Science Center started talking with possible fabricators about making full-sized models of various whale species. The Center wanted robotic models—models that moved.

Obviously, no one had designed an exhibit like this before, one in which moving whale models would swim among museum visitors in a simulated undersea environment. Quan stresses that its design was a cooperative effort: He spent long hours in planning with David Taylor of the Pacific Science Center and representatives of Sequoia Creative, Inc., who were hired to create the robotic whales.

The exhibit was a temporary one in 9000 sq. ft. of building No. 5, the structure the Center designated for temporary exhibits when it took over six buildings from what had been the Seattle World's Fair of 1962.

After six months in Seattle,

the exhibit was scheduled to travel to six other cities throughout the country. Quan visited other potential sites, taking along his measuring tape because he knew that getting a 35' whale model, even one that weighed only a ton or so, into a museum building should not be a design problem left to solve on the site. Because the minimum door size turned out to be 7' high and 6' wide, the whales were fabricated about 85 per cent of life-size, with fins flexible enough to fold down close to the bodies for squeezing into museums.

The final exhibit had five robotic whales arranged in the undersea world Quan created for them. Visitors entered the exhibit through a cave of artificial rocks, its ceiling

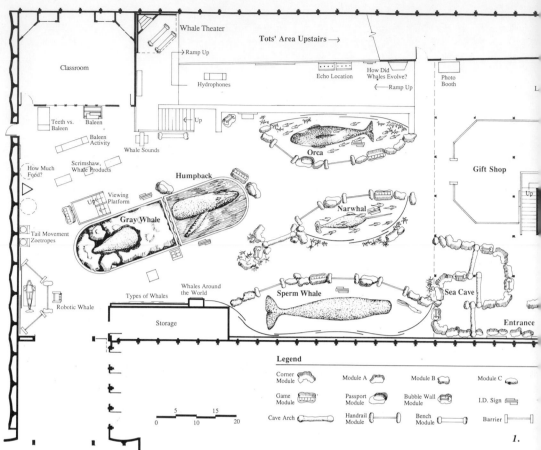

Legend

Corner Module · Module A · Module B · Module C · Game Module · Passport Module · Bubble Wall Module · I.D. Sign · Cave Arch Module · Handrail Module · Bench Module · Barrier

1.

2.

1. Floor plan.
2. Rendering of gray whale emerging from ice.
3. Robotic model of sperm whale.

3.

dropped to 8' by a camouflage net thrown over the rocks' upper ends. At a couple of places in the S-shaped cave, Quan placed bubble walls. Bubble walls are not really *walls*. The ones Quan used (six in all) are commercially available freestanding panels 8' high and 2' wide that are a sandwich of two ½"-thick sheets of acrylic with water inside. When a compressor blows bubbles through the water, it gives a sense of motion. In the cave, Quan elicited response from another human sense: As visitors entered, the sound of breaking waves washed over them.

From the cave, visitors emerged into the main exhibit space where five robotic whales (three were complete models, two were half models) swam in rocky grottoes. Directly in front of emerging visitors was a 32' sperm whale chasing a squid. Like all the other full models, the sperm whale was mounted on a C-shaped steel mount. The bottom of the C was supplied with castors on the floor while the top end of the C was

embedded in the whale's side and attached to its internal framework. Compressed-air apparatus inside the three full-model whales simulated a swimming motion, causing their tails to rise and fall as if they were pushing themselves through the water. And as their tails moved, the whales' jaws opened and closed and their eyes rolled.

Behind each whale was a wall of scrims stretched on wooden frames and painted in shades of dark blue and green. Quan mounted scrims at various positions in the exhibit, producing a murky effect through which visitors could dimly see other whales in the distance.

Gels revolving in front of the ceiling spots—some with blues and greens, some with linear or striated patterns—created a sense of motion as if the space were being swept by a current. Quan also gave each of the whales a basic color, darker blue-green for the sperm whale, which normally would be swimming in deeper water, and a lighter blue-green for the 25'

orca. Then he lighted each full-model whale from both below and above, so that its shadows filled the space.

Around each whale model was a rock barrier with 3'-high, clear acrylic panels substituting occasionally for the rocks so that small visitors could see up through them to the models. Ten different shapes were designed for the rocks, which come apart and nest for shipping. One rock shape had a flat shelf-like surface molded in near its top to hold edge-lighted graphic panels. Another had a molded-in surface for an information game consisting of a panel with a question screened on it; visitors lifted the panel to reveal the answer. Another type of rock had a flat shelf for a fold-out "passport station" (visitors could have Science Center passports stamped at each whale model) and space for an overhead light.

A 17' narwhal with a tusk almost 12' long was the third full-model whale; it swam on a 4' stand (so kids couldn't reach its tusk) among a school of molded fish hung on

monofilament from the ceiling grid. Fish schools swam at various open places in the exhibit and vacuum-formed kelp hung from rocks and overhead supports.

On the floor was a canvas floor scrim painted in blues, greens, and grays as if it were background. At out-of-way places, chicken wire formations rose beneath it to give a shape something like a sea floor.

Toward the rear of the space were the two half-models. The front half of a gray whale emerged from beneath an ice floe. Its head came out and its mouth opened. Visitors couldn't see the gray whale at first, unless they stood on a small viewing platform next to its habitat. Just in front of the gray whale, the front torso of a humpback whale (a 12'-long half-model) lay in bright light, as if on the surface of the water. The model spouted, rotated, and waved a flipper.

On the periphery were static exhibits in vitrines displaying parts of whale anatomy—a skull, for instance. One case showed products made from

4.

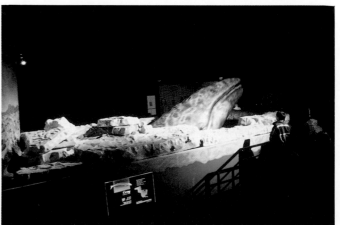

5.

whales, while others held interactive exhibits. In one of these, visitors could move whisks through a tank of water, scooping up buoyant particles to demonstrate the way baleen whales scoop up plankton. Overhead, suspended from the ceiling, were two large nets, one filled with milk cartons to illustrate how much milk a baby whale drinks in a day, the other with fish sandwich cartons to show how much a small whale eats in a day.

Against the end wall was a 10′ model of a robotic whale with its skin removed, revealing its structural framework and the pistons and hoses of its compressed air system. Visitors standing on a podium in front of the model could manipulate valve controls to make the model move. This was intended for fun and also to dispel any lingering doubts, if someone had them, about whether the models were real.

The exhibit sometimes frightened very small children. They entered through a dark cave into a watery-seeming dim space filled with moving

monsters, and often they cried. When this happened, docents suggested the children be taken to the mezzanine, where they could look out over the exhibit and see all the models at once, from a distance. From the mezzanine, the models seemed smaller and their surroundings less threatening. Hanging from the ceiling grid to just in front of the mezzanine railing was a 35′ gray whale skeleton, lighted from above. In case the skeleton was not distracting enough, Quan designed a tot's area on the mezzanine with tot-oriented games. For instance, built into the mezzanine floor was a board game, an idea he borrowed from the Monterey aquarium. On a giant board, fashioned like a Monopoly board, small children could keep track of migratory whales by moving them from the Northern Hemisphere to the Southern.

The exhibit had one other element, a video of five different whales filmed in the wild. This played on a 40″ screen in front of two benches on a small balcony off one side of the gallery.

6.

The designers and fabricators put the exhibit together in 18 months for $260,000. This did not include the Pacific Science Center's contribution of project management and installation. Nor did it include the $700,000 cost of the robotic whales. Quant says they revised the design four times to reduce the cost and in the end had to keep "the lighting, special-effects equipment, and controls to a

bare minimum." Despite all that, Quan's original concept emerged intact.

4. Exhibit overview.
5, 7. Robotic whales swim through space.
6. Early rendering.
8. Artifacts and specimens.

7.

8.

Client: Pacific Science Center (Seattle, WA)
Sponsor: Pacific Science Center
Design firm: Daniel Quan Design, San Francisco, CA
Designers: Daniel Quan, (principal designer), David Taylor (Pacific Science Center, project manager)
Consultants: San Francisco Light Works (lighting), San Francisco Maritime Historical Park (artifacts and photographs)
Fabricators: Sequoia Creative, Inc. (robotic whales), Dillon Works!, Inc. (Fiberglas rocks, squid, and other small fish), SuperScenics, Inc. (painted scrims, backdrops and floor drops), Pacific Science Center Exhibit Shop (exhibit modules, painting, installation)

Marine World and Maritime Wing

Marine World and the Maritime Wing at Norwalk, Connecticut's Maritime Center had an overall exhibit budget of $4.4 million. That figure for the design, fabrication, and installation of permanent exhibits had originally been $6 million; it was reduced by almost one-third because the renovation of the building to house them, a former foundry and manufacturing facility, ran over its budget. In a story as old as exhibition design itself, the exhibits had to absorb the overrun.

In the mid-19th century, the complex of buildings that is now the Maritime Center was Earle's Patent Steam Pumps and Engines Company. In one quick step, the renovation brought the complex into the heart of the late 20th century. Besides the exhibitions, the buildings now house an IMAX theater, space for research on boats, a fast-food outlet, a small gift shop, and offices.

The impetus for exhibition design came from a 1970s study suggesting that any renovation of South Norwalk include a museum showcase with an aquarium and natural history exhibits. What resulted is, indeed, a showcase despite the drastic budget cuts; the Maritime Center is already Connecticut's third largest tourist attraction.

Joseph A. Wetzel Associates, the Boston design firm that designed the exhibits for Marine World and the Maritime Wing, started the project with a feasibility study. Even before Graham Gund Architects signed on to do the renovation, the Wetzel designers had established an exhibit story line,

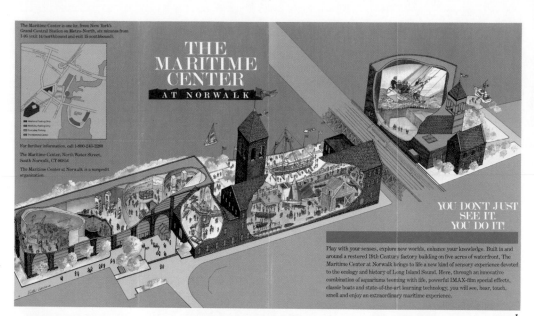

1.

2.

3.

4.

1. Folder explains Maritime Center.
2. Model of aquarium tanks.
3. Model of exhibit space.
4. Maritime Center exterior.
5. Interior portion of indoor-outdoor sea lion pool.

Photos:
Joseph A. Wetzel Associates (Figs. 2, 3, 7, 8, 11, 13, 15 & 16)
Steve Rosenthal (Figs. 4-6)
Cymie Payne (Figs. 12 & 14)

planned the space, and developed a concept of building flow for the exhibits.

What the Center wanted was an exhibition program showing how people interact with Long Island Sound, which the Norwalk area borders, and a presentation of the Sound's marine life.

For the marine portion of the exhibit, the designers envisioned a tour through the area's ecosystems. Their design, arranged as if a visitor were walking from the Maritime Center to the middle of the Atlantic, leads visitors from salt marsh through tidal pools to the shallow water of the Sound and then to the depths of the Atlantic, the Gulf Stream, and the Caribbean. The designers decided to make the traffic here flow one way, guiding visitors in part with color and light from the brightly lit green of the salt marshes to the more dimly lit, deeper blues of the open ocean. In this Marine World section of the exhibit are 10,300 sq. ft. of open floor space, not counting support spaces behind the wall tanks, or the tanks themselves, of which there are 21 ranging in capacity from 150 to 110,000 gallons.

Visitors enter through a space devoted to the salt marsh. Here, against a curved wall cupping the exhibit space, the designers mounted a 160-sq.-ft. mural of a Long Island Sound salt marsh. They couldn't glue the canvas mural directly to the wall because they wanted to be able to save it if the space were ever redesigned. Instead, they covered the wall with a foam substance, behind whose edges (after it hardened) they tucked the mural, holding it in

place with metal strips. In the open area in front of the mural, they spaced five salt marsh exhibits, each installed in a ceiling-high square pillar measuring 3' to a side. The display section—a clear acrylic tank 2½' high—is set into the pillar at eye level. For easy viewing, graphic panels just below the display tanks are angled toward the viewer at 45 degrees. One pillar, for instance, contains artificial spartina grass, and the information panel (graphics over a green background view of a salt marsh) explains how the grass provides a cover for animal life both above and below the water line and how the grass itself is an important link in the food chain.

One pillar holds a computer game. Visitors touch a video screen to determine how an imbalance might occur among the number of fish, birds, and insects, depending on the amount of fishing. If fishing increases, the number of birds decreases, and so on.

A 540-sq.-ft. mural of a Long Island beach follows the curved wall of the intertidal area. When staff members are present, visitors can step up to a low, open fiberglass tank (a three-quarter-circle shape with a 16' diameter), reach in and pull out a species of intertidal dweller—a sand dollar, for instance, or an oyster, or a sea urchin. The designers called this tank the touch-tank and, as might be expected, it holds visitors' attention longer than the regular fish tanks do—up to 10 or 15 minutes. Always available at the touch-tank is a docent or someone on the museum staff to control the touching and

5.

6.

7.   8.

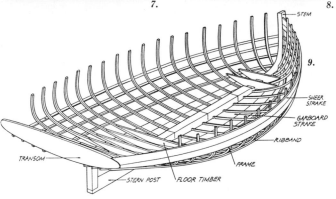

9.

STEM

SHEER
STRAKE

GARBOARD
STRAKE

RIBBAND

TRANSOM

FRAME

STERN POST   FLOOR TIMBER

10. FIGURE-OF-EIGHT KNOT

The figure-of-eight knot has been called the perfect knot because of
its symmetry. It is used as a stopper knot to prevent a line from running
out the end of a block. It does not jam and can be easily untied.

1   2   3   4

explain what is being touched.
When the museum personnel
are not there, panels cover the
tank.

Also in the intertidal area is
an open re-creation of a tidal
marsh behind a 30″-high and
15′-long acrylic panel. At a
waist-high podium just in front
of the tidal marsh, visitors can
control an underwater camera
in the marsh and watch the
images on an overhead video
screen.

Angling off behind the marsh
are wall cases. On one side, a
case holds a re-creation of a
beach at low tide, and on the
other, a case shows the beach
at high tide. Graphic panels
mounted on 2″-diameter pipe
rail offer explanatory text.

In the Long Island Sound
area, five triangular pylons hold
interactive devices that help
explain fish. One, for instance,
has a video camera behind a
plastic bubble on one side of the
pylon; another camera is
similarly mounted on another
side, and the third side has
camera controls. Visitors can
maneuver the two cameras,
watching the images on two
video screens, to get an idea of
how a fish's eyes record
different images. On a blue
metal stand among the pylons is
a 7′-long simulated fish skeleton
with two short metal rods
protruding from its skull.
Visitors who grab these rods,
and then whip the skeleton from
side to side, can see how it
undulates, just as it would if the
fish were swimming. Six wall
tanks show fish communities
encountering various bottom
conditions, i.e., rocky ledges or
sand. One of the tanks, built in
an oval, has a school of fish,
schooling.

The lighting grows dimmer
and the wall colors tend toward
deeper blue in the next space,
the open ocean, dominated by
the Center's largest tank,
kidney-shaped, 24′ at its widest
and 46′ long. At the back of the
tank, in the kidney's inward
curve, are video screens.
Visitors sit on carpeted steps in
front of the screens to watch
videos of the open ocean.

As noted, this exhibit has
21 tanks. Above them are
graphic headers, perhaps 6′ off
the floor, "like a newspaper
headline," hawking what the
tank illustrates, says Howard
Litwak, project manager for
Wetzel Associates. Beneath
each tank on a triangular
lightbox, with a water-tinted
image tilting 45 degrees toward
the viewer, are nine vertical
inches of text explaining the
tank.

For the Maritime Center's
Maritime wing, Wetzel
Associates designed 8000 sq.
ft. of exhibits on the commercial
history of Long Island. Part of
it, as might be expected, is
devoted to the oyster, which is
an important part of the Sound's
history. In a re-creation of a
working oyster bar, visitors can
sit and sample the Sound's
oysters. Boating exhibits
occupy the rest of the space.
Five interactive displays enable
visitors to test their
understanding of boating and
boating devices, such as Loran,
radar, compass, depth sounder,
and radio. The interactive
displays are located in wooden
boxes painted with white
automotive paint and mounted
on white-painted steel columns
12″ in diameter, 21″ off the
ground.

In an exhibit that Howard

Litwak describes as "part work space and part stage set," a boat-builder works at his craft. Selected for both his boat-building skills and his ability to communicate with visitors, the builder explains what he's doing. In front of his space, defining and protecting it, are lectern-style graphic panels—4' wide and 1' deep—installed about 3' off the floor. A sandwich of acrylic over wired glass protects the graphics. Here, and throughout both Marine World and the Maritime Wing, the designers specified Times Roman typeface.

Upstairs, overlooking these spaces, the designers positioned similar graphic panels on a railing. Just beyond the railing they hung six or seven boats from the ceiling. These include a dugout canoe and a windsurfer, boats used on the Sound at one time or another.

Schematic design for the Center's exhibits took 5 months. Design development and construction documents took 12 months and fabrication and installation, 20 months.

6, 7. Graphic panels have wood slab supports.
8. Boats used on Long Island Sound hang from Maritime Wing ceiling. Graphics explaining them are on balcony railing.
9, 10. Graphic details.
11. Piloting display lets visitors test maritime devices such as radar, Loran, and depth sounders.
12, 14. Touch tanks.
13. Visitors can grab a handle on skull of this skeletal fish and move skeleton to simulate movement of swimming fish.
15. Pylons hold tanks illustrating the ecology of Long Island Sound.
16. Circular tank with schooling fish.

11.

12.

13.

14.

15.

16.

Client: The Maritime Center at Norwalk (South Norwalk, CT)
Sponsors: Norwalk Redevelopment Authority; Junior League of Stamford-Norwalk; Oceanic Society; Norwalk Seaport Association
Design firm: Joseph A. Wetzel Associates, Inc., Boston, MA
Consultants: EXPLUS, Inc., Duncan Bert (detailing); Gallegos Lighting Design, Pat Gallegos (lighting); Graham Gund Architects, Don Self (architecture)
Fabricators: General Exhibits and Displays, Inc.; The Larson Co.; Reynolds Polymer Technology, Inc.; Aquatic Environments; Ray Museum Studios; New England Technology Group, Inc.; the Mariano Brothers; Pallas Photo Labs, Inc.; Heddi Seibel; Roger Hambidge; Julia Ferguson

Masterworks of Louis Comfort Tiffany

In his 27 years at the Smithsonian's National Museum of American Art, Val Lewton had never designed an exhibit so complex. The museum wanted a sumptuous setting for some 75 objects designed by Louis Comfort Tiffany—lamps, jewelry, vases, mosaic panels, and windows. Some of the exhibit's 11 windows were 11' or 12' high and some of the small objects such as jeweled boxes, bottles, vases, a paperweight, an inkwell, and jewelry were less than 6". It took Lewton about a year to design the exhibit and see it in place, including two months for construction and installation.

In all, the exhibit spread through 7000 sq. ft. in five galleries of the Museum of American Art's Renwick Gallery, which was built in 1859 with 25' ceilings in French Second Empire style. Lewton decided to keep the gallery's basic architectural structure but to give the gallery rooms the feel of a Tiffany design. He did this by incorporating a few simple elements such as velvet draperies and furniture designed by Lewton to look like furniture from Tiffany's time (1847-1932). Lewton felt that the settings Tiffany designed for himself in the places he worked and lived justified this simplicity. Anyway, the exhibit budget—even though it eventually ran to about $95,000 from the original $75,000— didn't allow for anything more elaborate.

Lewton first had the rooms painted a unifying brownish gray and the floors covered with a plush teal-green carpet with a 10" mustard-green border. Over the windows he hung velvet draperies on wooden rings from painted metal pipes. In the first two galleries, these draperies were a red wine color and in the last gallery, gold.

Lewton displayed almost everything openly, placing only small decorative objects like vases and jewelry in cases. He covered the Plexiglas edges of the cases he did use (mostly borrowed from the Revere show at the Smithsonian's Sackler Museum) with brass trim to make them look like period glass vitrines. He continued the feeling of luxury, achieved through simple means, by making all the labels etched bronze with Seraph typeface.

Initially, Lewton considered grouping items by category, all lamps together, for instance, and windows displayed with other windows. But it quickly became obvious that the windows were so large they each should be placed alone, at the end of major sight lines, if they weren't going to overpower one another. Another idea had been to have all the windows visible from two sides, to guide visitors down corridors brightly lit as if by daylight and let them look through the windows to the galleries' interiors. This was rejected because there wasn't enough space.

Instead, everything was mixed together as if in a Tiffany-designed interior. To display Tiffany table lamps, Lewton (with Martin Kotler, the museum's cabinetmaker) designed tables in two heights, 30" and 35", that looked vaguely like tables Tiffany had owned. Most of these he placed on low platforms made of Masonite

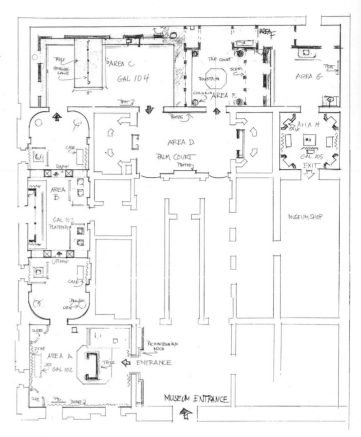

TIFFANY EXHIBITION SCHEMATIC
SCALE
⅛" = 1'

LEGEND 1. ━━━ POCHE' LINE INDICATES PARTITION WALL CONT.
2. ▦ SHADED AREA INDICATES PLATFORMS
3. ∿∿ INDICATES DRAPERY

1.

1. Floor plan.
2,3. Richardson-like arch frames exhibit entrance with velvet drape and title plaque beyond.
4. Three Tiffany-designed lamps hang on specially designed wrought iron bar above 15' table which simulates one of Tiffany's.

2.

3.

4.

5. *Looking through gallery to Tiffany stained glass window.*
6. *Ceramic container.*
7. *Courtyard with 4-panel magnolia and wisteria window, and vase designed like one used by Tiffany in his courtyard fountain.*

5.

(painted a dark gray-green) over plywood with a stained oak border. Around the platforms, Lewton placed barriers of his design—waist-high wrought-iron posts, given an Art Nouveau look, and stained oak railings. These railings held the bronze labels.

In the lamps, Lewton used low-wattage bulbs in different colors—blue, yellow, white, rose—to highlight the fixtures.

To show some hanging lamps to good advantage, Lewton designed a large table, 8′ by 15′, bigger and less complicated than one of Tiffany's, and gave it a gray-green Masonite center with a stained oak trim like the platforms near it. Lewton put a

velvet runner on the table and an arrangement of dried leaves. Above, he suspended three Tiffany hanging lamps from a 13″-long wrought-iron bar that he had fabricated to match one Tiffany had in his Long Island home, Laurelton Hall.

"Laurelton Hall had almost an arts and crafts look," says Lewton. "The windows were set directly into the walls in shallow niches." Lewton mounted his Tiffany windows in frames, setting them into the wall in front of fluorescent lights diffused through mylar. One, he set in front of a gallery window so it shone with natural light. And one, the magnolia and wisteria window with its four

89″-by-37″ panels, he set in a courtyard, where it was visible both from the adjacent gallery and from the courtyard.

With the design help of Ethan Cohen, a summer intern, Lewton re-created one of Tiffany's two courtyards at Laurelton Hall. Or most of it. They couldn't find capitals for the columns that rose to the corners of the simulated skylight, so they had to design their own. Lewton found a glassblower who created the special clear-glass vase that stands 2′ high in the center of the fountain. He copied one Tiffany had in *his* fountain, although Tiffany's was bigger and stained red from years of

immersion in water. "It took me a week to get the pump working right," says Lewton of the pump that filled the vase to overflowing, creating the fountain's effect. Lewton used Mexican wall tile on the floor and walls of the fountain courtyard. "We couldn't afford more expensive tile," he says, "and, for a six-month installation, the wall tile held up fine under foot. It just was slippery for a day, until it was walked on some."

Visitors entered the exhibit through a Richardsonian-like arch that Lewton had built around the gallery's entrance. Lewton wanted to dramatize the move from the museum's

6.

7.

sun-drenched lobby, which has, he says, an "outside feeling," into the exhibit where the feeling was very much of being inside. Through the entrance arch, one saw a tile plaque mounted on a wine-colored velvet drapery. Lewton farmed out the plaque's design and construction. Letters were cut from Plexiglas and mounted on a Plexiglas sheet; then, the whole plaque was painted to look like bronze. One of the Casebook jurors called it "disappointing." Just past this entrance plaque was an element of the exhibit that *Lewton* thought disappointing. On angled walls built into two corners of the room he installed

a back-projected slide show. Three projectors lined up slides vertically, filling wood-framed screens in each corner with images of flowers and Tiffany-designed details. What disappointed Lewton was the cost ($10,000) and the fact that the projectors made a distracting clack—when they were working, that is. They kept breaking down and, because the museum rarely uses slide projectors and has no one to maintain them, they tended to stay down for long periods.

Throughout the exhibit, Lewton displayed potted palms and ferns in wicker baskets "because that's what the

museum had," and, in terra-cotta pots in corners, lots of bamboo shoots, which the staff horticulturist cut at Washington's National Zoo. "It looked like clouds of gray in the corners," says Lewton. In the courtyard fountain were aquatic plants. All this greenery helped achieve the feel of interiors in the Tiffany era.

Visitors wound through the galleries and, from the last room, Lewton had a door that opened into the gift shop. Thus, for one of the first times at the Renwick, visitors had no choice but to exit past display racks of exhibit-related items for sale. As a result, weekend gift shop sales increased tenfold.

Client: National Museum of American Art, Smithsonian Institution (Washington, DC)
Sponsor: Tiffany, Inc.
Design firm: Office of Design and Production, National Museum of American Art
Designers: Val Lewton; Robyn Kennedy (graphics)
Design assistance: Victor Korenev, Ethan Cohen, Martin Kotler
Consultants: Jeremy Adamson (curator, National Museum of American Art), Alastair Duncan (guest curator)
Fabricators: Victor Korenev, Ron Pacci, Nelson Beck Inc., Black Rose Forge, National Museum of American Art Office of Design and Production

The Intimate World of Alexander Calder

"Calder was a maker," says Dorothy Globus, coordinator of exhibitions at the Cooper-Hewitt Museum, the Smithsonian Institution's National Museum of Design. Jo Ann Secor of Lee H. Skolnick Architecture and Design, the firm that designed this exhibition of Calder's work, calls him a "gadgeteer." "Calder always carried pliers and wire to whip out and create something—a brass pin, door latch, or wire figure," she says.

The Cooper-Hewitt wanted the exhibit to show more than just Calder's art, the mobiles, paintings, and stabiles for which he is best known. "He was always tinkering, creating beautiful and useful objects, things like lamps and wire figures, and he would use these in his home," says Lee Skolnick. "The exhibit was not so much about Calder's art as about one man making beautiful and useful objects."

The exhibit Skolnick designed took over the second floor of the Cooper-Hewitt, which is housed in Andrew Carnegie's former mansion in New York City. The exhibit became a

statement about Calder's life and work shown in the context of the objects he made and lived with.

In all, the exhibit took up about 5000 sq. ft. spread through eight rooms. As visitors went up the stairs, they saw, on the landing, a large Calder mobile, and at the top of the stairs, against a wall painted yellow-orange, a color Calder frequently used, a photo blowup of Calder and one of his wire sculptures, "Spring."

Throughout the exhibit, the designers used Calder's colors: bright red, yellow, orange and blue, what Dorothy Globus has called "orangey-red, brilliant yellow, and almost iridescent blue." Then, a neutral gray was employed as a backdrop and a way of setting the exhibit off from the rest of the museum. The exhibit was made to fit the existing space, using the existing lighting. "We built almost no new partitions" says Jo Ann Secor.

The spaces were those of the old Carnegie mansion. "We're in a house," Dorothy Globus comments matter-of-factly. "The second floor has a center

1.

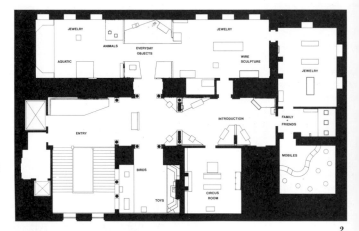

2.

④ CENTER HALL NORTH WALL ELEVATION

3.

1. Preliminary rendering.
2. Floor plan.
3. Elevation.
4. Calder birds fly in front of exhibit title.
5,6. Photo blowups of Calder's studio and Calder at work behind some of the innumerable pieces he fashioned.

4.

5.

hall with [what were] bedrooms and bathrooms off it."

In the center hall, Skolnick set up an orientation area, what he called a "didactic spine." Visitors moved into it past either side of a painting Calder had done of his studio, mounted on an off-white panel. This orientation area had a series of panel-backed platforms arranged at different angles to each other and to the walls. On the panels, each of which was painted in a bold Calder color, were black-and-white photo blowups in different sizes (mostly about 3′ by 4′) showing Calder at work, his friends and family, and offering glimpses of his studio and home. In front of these photos, in cases set into platforms, were small Calder-designed objects—jewelry, toys, sculpture, and so on. The idea was to show Calder's creations in the light of his personality and the people who influenced his everyday life. One area, for instance, emphasized his whimsy, another his mechanical bent, another his obsessiveness, another his universality, and yet another, his family and friends.

The show originated in Paris, at the Musée des Arts Décoratifs, and its curator

6.

there, Daniel Marchesseau, was guest curator for the Cooper-Hewitt installation. Dorothy Globus saw the Paris installation and realized right off she wanted to do it differently and that to do so she needed more of Calder's work. Back in New York, she went around to members of Calder's family, many of whom live in the New York area, and solicited items to include in the Cooper-Hewitt's exhibit. As a result, the exhibit had a richness it could not otherwise have had, and it possessed, too—perhaps owing more to the arrangement of the Carnegie Mansion's spaces than to any machinations of the designers—a seeming randomness in the way it could be approached, a spontaneity, that would probably have delighted Calder. Visitors would come up the stairs and, ignoring the orientation area, go directly into one of the peripheral rooms, usually to the one with a videotape of Calder and his circus.

In one room off the central hallway were stabiles and mobiles (moving lazily in the gentle wash of a fan), against vivid yellow walls. This yellow and white room had, Skolnick says, "a sunny, natural, un-museum-like feeling, almost like being outdoors." In this room was a serpentine case snaking 16′ through the space. Left from another show, the case displayed Calder jewelry and hand-held stabiles.

As noted, many visitors started with the room housing Calder's circus—small circus figures and objects of wire, wood, and metal that Calder would make perform. The video in the circus room, of Calder

7.

8.

7. Calder fish suspended in aquarium-like case.
8. Exuberant examples of Calder's wire sculpture.
9-12. A few of the thousands of useful and playful objects Calder was constantly creating—toys, jewelry, sculpture, etc.

and his wife performing the circus, was borrowed from the Whitney Museum, where it's on permanent display. Skolnick set up the video screen at one end of the room with 15 or 20 seats.

Other rooms held what the designers called "tableaus" of rooms in Calder's home. Because the museum was leery of re-creating Calder's home or work spaces, feeling that that approach might detract from what the exhibit was trying to emphasize, the designers abstracted these spaces. They designed tableaus of his living room and kitchen. Visitors entered the living room through black clapboard walls, like the black clapboards Calder had on his house in Roxbury, Connecticut. Inside the room, the walls, to 8′ above the floor, were stuccoed and topped by wood moldings. On floor-planked platforms, the room displayed things Calder had designed and used in his home.

In one room several of Calder's wire "drawings" of heads were hung from the ceiling, close enough to a wall so that they rested against it, simulating real drawings, 8′ off the floor. In a space just beyond the living room tableau, the designers turned a wall case into an aquarium (6′ deep, 16′ wide, 10′ high). In it, they mounted a sampling of Calder fish, some (colored glass mobiles) suspended on monofilament, turning to fan-pushed air currents.

In all, the exhibit displayed some 300 Calder items. The designers specified an ITC Novarese typeface, using it in medium and ultra weight and in medium italic for interpretive panels.

They designed the show in 3½ months. During its run, they were delighted by the public's response—watching "people's faces light up" as they moved through the stately Carnegie mansion rooms.

9.

10.

11.

Client: Cooper-Hewitt Museum (New York, NY)
Sponsors: American Express Co.; Andy Warhol Foundation for the Visual Arts; Helena Rubinstein Foundation; Smithsonian Institution Special Exhibition Fund
Design firm: Lee H. Skolnick Architecture + Design, New York, NY
Designers: Lee H. Skolnick (principal), Diane Alexander (design assistant), Jo Ann Secor (LHS Museum services director), Julie Chwatsky (exhibit assistant), Dorothy T. Globus (coordinator of exhibits, Cooper-Hewitt), Daniel Marchesseau (guest curator), Mentyka/Schlott Design (graphic design)

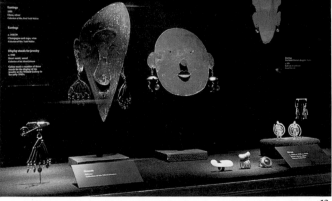

12.

Zenga: Brushstrokes of Enlightenment

As visitors entered the first of three galleries at Charlotte, North Carolina's, Mint Museum of Art, where this traveling exhibit of some 70 Japanese scrolls stopped for two months, they confronted two Japanese characters representing the words *Zen ga*, which means Zen painting. The words, appearing on the back wall of a specially designed alcove with a floor of two tatami mats, were painted in a cream color behind the show title "Zenga: Brushstrokes of Enlightenment," printed in English in Janson typeface. The Japanese characters were subtle, blending with the soft gray of the 10′-high partition on which they were painted, so that only careful lighting from the galleries' ceiling spots made them stand out.

Subtlety was a hallmark of the exhibit design and so was simplicity. Daniel Gottlieb, who headed the Mint Museum design team, wanted to display the scrolls in an atmosphere of calm and order. Almost all the elements of his exhibition design contributed to that feeling. Colors, textures, lights, even the koto (flute) music that filtered softly through the exhibit, were both subtle and calming.

To isolate the scrolls, to give each its own space, and—not incidentally—to protect them, Gottlieb designed separate fir frames for most, covering them with Plexiglas. But he left the backs open, so the scrolls hung against the wall. Two frames held two scrolls rather than the usual one. Each scroll had a 4″ border of wall on each side between it and its frame and, in some cases, between it and

another scroll. He achieved a uniformity of sorts, a "graphic presence," by selecting scrolls which were roughly similar in height and placing them in frames that varied only in width.

Using three colors chosen to give the walls of the galleries a warm glow (different colors in different exhibit sections), Gottlieb painted the walls within the scroll frames one of the two colors that weren't being used on the wall in that section. Doing this, Gottlieb says, pushed the scroll forward, isolating it from the wall slightly. Not surprisingly, the three colors he chose were calming: salmon; light, warm

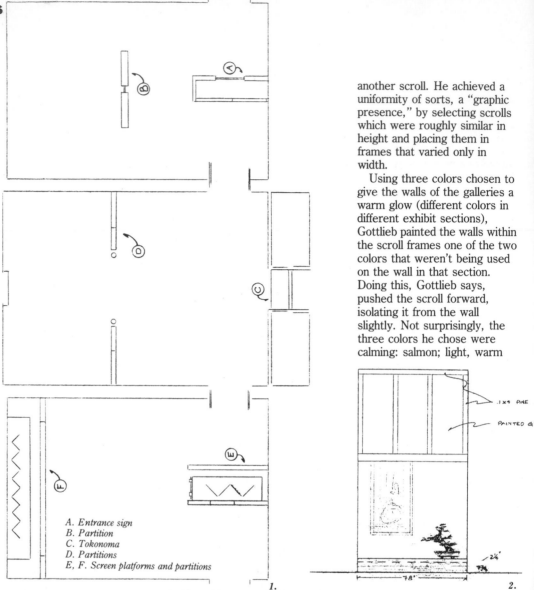

A. Entrance sign
B. Partition
C. Tokonoma
D. Partitions
E, F. Screen platforms and partitions

1.

2.

3.

1. Floor plan. Exhibit entrance at top.
2. Preliminary elevation of small meditation chamber with bonsai tree.
3. Exhibit title at entrance in Japanese characters behind show title in English.
4. Meditation Chamber in exhibit (C in floor plan).
5. Scrolls in frames and partition wall with Japanese-like gates. Posts are trunks of cedar trees uprooted by Hurricane Hugo.

gray; and a slightly whiter gray.

The exhibit had four sections, each centered around a separate theme. The first concerned Daruma, a Zen teacher. The second showed scrolls of Zen heroes; the third, Zen teachings (such as satori, aspects of human experience that lead to spiritual awakening); and the fourth, Zen calligraphy. In seven or eight places over the scroll, using transfer type, Gottlieb put koan, Zen riddles, such as "What is the sound of one hand clapping?"

On the walls, blocks of text 14″ wide, also in transfer type (Janson typeface), introduced each section.

At one end of the second gallery, Gottlieb designed a traditional meditation chamber, or tokonomo, raised a foot above the floor on a platform covered by a 3′-by-6′ tatami mat. On the mat were a bonsai tree on a carved wooden stand and a traditional Japanese floral arrangement, or ikebana. On the wall at the rear of the chamber was one of the show's scrolls illuminated from the top by a fluorescent light shining through rice paper and, from the right side, through a round rice-paper window. Gottlieb says he wouldn't have known that tradition requires that the round window, which represents the moon, be located on the right had it not been for Masachi (Mike) Oshita, a Japanese gardener he found working and living in Monroe, North Carolina. Gottlieb brought Oshita to the Mint to create a 2000-sq.-ft Zen garden in front of the museum, one Gottlieb wanted as both an introduction and an adjunct to

4.

5.

the exhibit.

Certainly, the tokonomo added to the exhibit's prevailing sense of calm. Although most visitors did not realize it, they could step up into the tokonomo if they wished. Japanese visitors, recognizing the tokonomo for what it was, would politely leave their shoes on the gallery floor, step onto the tatami, and stand there quietly for a while.

Gottlieb broke up the space in the galleries by designing free-standing walls, which he had constructed in the center of the first gallery, and partitions that extended from the side walls of the second gallery to form a gateway. Throughout the space, he used Japanese architectural elements such as rice-paper screens, some of which he borrowed from a Japanese restaurant in Charlotte and some of which Gottlieb, who has a degree in furniture design, designed himself. For example, to create the gateway in the center gallery, he stood the slender trunks of two cedar trees (uprooted by Hurricane Hugo) at the inner ends of the two partitions that he extended into the room from either side

wall. On top of the partitions he placed 1'-high rice-paper-backed gates that ran the 12' from each cedar pole to the wall.

In all, the galleries offered 5000 sq. ft. of floor space. This also helped maintain the atmosphere of calm, for Gottlieb could give each scroll enough space to keep it from competing with its neighbors.

At three places in the galleries, Gottlieb positioned low, slatted, backless benches, also of his own design, on which visitors sat quietly and gazed at the scrolls and at the exhibit in general. Gottlieb feels that the exhibit "achieved a Zen-like atmosphere—contemplative and balanced." The proof, he says, was that visitors lingered much longer (up to 30 minutes) in the Zen galleries than they did in other Mint Museum exhibits. "People," he feels, "were comfortable enough to sit and do nothing."

Gottlieb had thought about a Zen garden at the museum for a long time. Masachi Oshita made the one in front of the Mint traditional, tracing, in its sand, various patterns of grooves and ridges, and grouping three kinds of rocks: large boulders selected for their form and artistic shape, white river pebbles, and reddish clay stones of remarkable uniformity of size, texture, and color. The Charlotte Garden Club sponsored the garden.

The designers and fabricators put the exhibit together in 3 months on a budget of $25,000.

The Casebook jurors called it "elegant."

6. Scroll next to recessed Japanese-like detail.
7. Screen platform and partition in Gallery 3.
8. Detail of 2,000-sq.-ft. Zen garden built in front of museum as adjunct to the exhibit.

Client: Mint Museum of Art (Charlotte, NC)
Corporate sponsor: Osuma Machinery, Inc.
Design firm: Mint Museum of Art Design Department
Designers: Daniel Gottlieb (head of design and installation), Emily Blanchard (graphics)
Consultants: Masachi Oshita (Zen garden), Charles L. Mo (curator)
Fabricators: Kurt Warnke (chief preparator), Mitchell Francis, Carol Ambrose; Leah Blackburn, William Lipscom (independent contractors)

Tony Walton:
Designing for Stage and Screen

Tony Walton has designed sets for Broadway shows and Hollywood films for more than 30 years, including *A Funny Thing Happened on the Way to the Forum* (both play and film), *Grand Hotel* (play), and *Mary Poppins* (film). In fact, Walton's work is so extensive and significant that one of the problems facing exhibit designer Lucian Leone of the Leone Design Group was how to help Walton edit models, photos, and drawings of his work to fit a 1600-sq.-ft. temporary exhibit space at the American Museum of the Moving Image in New York City (Astoria, Queens).

The space gave Leone other problems. "It was essentially an elongated shoe box," he says, "with a single way in and out." One entire wall of the 100′ length was lined with windows. Moreover, the museum is in a building that was once a film studio and looks like an old mill or factory. Leone wanted an exhibit system that would suit both the building and Tony Walton's work.

Because the budget was only $40,000 for design and production, he wanted something inexpensive; because he had only three weeks in which to install it, he did not want to spend a lot of time sawing and painting, making a mess that would have to be cleaned up.

So he went looking for an inexpensive, handsome exhibit framework and came up with Impac. Impac is a wire-mesh grid system commonly used in merchandising, and, says Leone, "Its mesh looks industrial so it fit the building, and it is minimal, high-tech, and esthetically right for what I was

1. Low-cost wire mesh grid system holds photos, sketches, models, and artifacts from Tony Walton's set designs.
2. Theater set model for Death of a Salesman.
3. Model figures of characters from film The Wiz.

2.

3.

trying to do." Besides, it came with simple plastic straps so the designers could fasten the 4'-by-8' Impac modules together. Then, using equally simple off-the-shelf hooks and clamps, they could fasten to the mesh the lightboxes, shelves, and text panels needed to display Walton's work. No screwing, hammering, drilling, or sawing. No painting. No mess.

Leone arranged his mesh grid down both sides of the room, covering the windows with miniblinds. Then, he lined up 4'-wide sections of the grid at right angles to the wall on either side of the room, punctuating the exhibit at four points. These partitions and the end wall created what were essentially five rooms, one for each of the exhibit's sections. Visitors moved from one wall to the opposite wall in each section instead of following the exhibit down one long wall and back along the other.

Leone placed some of Walton's stage-set models in individual Plexiglas cases on a table of 35"-wide white shelving board and set others in light boxes in back of a black Sintra sheet. Sintra is a Swiss vinyl that comes in about a ⅜" thickness. Leone cut windows in the vinyl, filled them with clear Plexiglas and put lightboxes with Walton's set-models behind the Plexi. A plastic collar something like a shower-curtain hook slipped through slits cut in the Sintra to hold it to the wire-mesh grid.

Leone used Sintra for text panels, too, cutting them from white ½"-thick sheets, silk-screening on the text in Times Roman ("classical, easy to read"), and hanging the panels

from the wire mesh with what he wryly calls "minimalist hanging devices"; i.e., S-hooks.

The designers tried to make the texts sound like Tony Walton talking, describing his work in his own words and cadences, like an "oral history."

Sandwiching Walton prints between two Plexiglas layers held at the corners by Swiss clamps, Leone used S-hooks, fastened over the strings that held the clamps in place, to hang the prints from the mesh grid. At the end of the room, he mounted renderings directly to the wall with mirror clips that held the Plexiglas sandwiches and screwed to the wall. Models of figures from the play *The Wiz* stand in front of the wall in a Plexiglas case, raised on a base of Impac wire grid.

Tony Walton's lighting designer, Michael Lincoln, came in to do the lighting. In an assignment very different from lighting a Broadway stage set, Lincoln mounted small lights, some with color filters, above the models. He lighted the rest of the items with the museum's track lighting system, to which he added some of his own fixtures and colored gels.

The Leone Design Group put the exhibit together in 4½ months.

The Casebook jurors called the exhibit "terrific."

4. Theater set model for Anything Goes.
5. Photos mounted directly on wall and on Plexiglas panel.
6. Photos in Plexiglas sandwich hung on wire grid with S-hooks.
7. Models in Plexiglas cases.
8. Models in light boxes behind openings in Sintra sheet.

4.

5.   6.

7.

8.

Client: American Museum of the Moving Image (Astoria, Queens, NY), Donald Albrecht, curator of exhibitions
Design firm: Leone Design Group, Larchmont, NY
Designers: Lucian J. Leone (design director), Nancy Zink White (senior graphic designer), Sally A. Leone (exhibition coordinator)
Consultants: Michael Lincoln (lighting)
Fabricator: RH Guest, Inc.

63/Exhibition Design

Ecos

Ecos is a permanent environmental exhibit at the Museum for Education in the Hague, the Netherlands. The museum and the Amsterdam firm hired to design the exhibit—Samenwerkende Ontwerpers—discussed it for a year. They wanted an exhibit that would snap people out of the somnolent state which they feared the word "environmental" is beginning to induce. They wanted something spritely, immediate, alive. But after a year, they still had no idea how to go about it.

Finally, the Museum turned Samenwerkende Ontwerpers loose. "We were given carte blanche," says Marianne Vos, who headed the design team. In essence, SO became its own client.

The designers decided to focus on the environmental concerns of the home, which, of course, have ramifications that reach far beyond home, and to do this they designed a 300-sq.-ft. stage-set house. They painted bold black lines on its beige walls to delineate rooms, which they labeled in bold black letters on its concrete floors—bedroom, kitchen, dining room, and so on. Then they brought the space alive with bright red and yellow accent colors on cabinet doors and furniture.

In the dining room, which became the exhibit's hub, they set up wooden benches in right-angled configurations in front of what would have been the room's windows. Instead, these window spaces became screens for slide shows. And the house and the things in it became part of the show. The refrigerator door pops open to reveal a laboratory. A cow comes out of the living room cuckoo clock, and a dog fabricated with a side section removed to show his intestines drops from the ceiling. In the bathroom, a cutaway toilet flushes, its innards exposed. In the bedroom, a bed mounted high on the wall begins to creak and sway when the subject of overpopulation comes up.

Around the house are handwritten texts in red script—on a door, a mirror, a wall—explaining the environment of a home, how a home converts raw materials and energy into products and waste, and how energy—gas, water, electricity, oil—are continually used with consequences for the outside environment.

Marianne Vos worked with a writer/biologist, Midas Dekkers, on the storyboard for the audiovisual show. Her most difficult job, she says, was finding fabricators for the props.

It took a year to design and install the exhibit, following the initial year of inconclusive discussions.

2.

1.

Doorsnede D-D'
3.

Doorsnede A-A'
4.

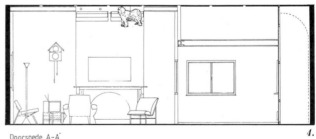
Doorsnede B-B'
5.

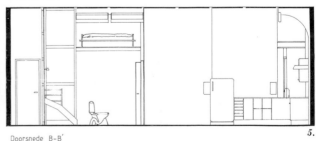
Doorsnede C-C'
6.

1. Cover of exhibit brochure.
2. Floor plan.
3-6. Elevations.
7. Kitchen and living room with cutaway dog model hung from ceiling.
8. Bathroom with cutaway toilet.
9. Kitchen with refrigerator door that opened automatically during exhibit.
10-11. Cover and interior of exhibit folder.
12. Visitors watch slide show in dining room.

7.

10.

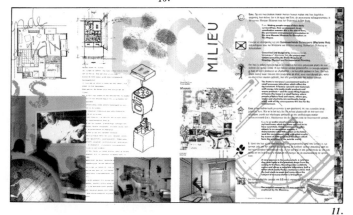

11.

8.

9.

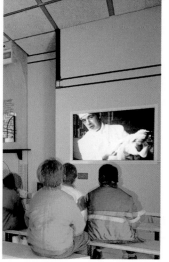

12.

Client: Museum for Education (The Hague, the Netherlands)
Sponsor: Ministry of Housing, Physical and Environmental Planning
Design firm: Samenwerkende Ontwerpers, Amsterdam
Designers: Marianne Vos (concept, design), Andre Toet (design), Josephine Oudijn (interior design)
Consultants: Rob Hauser (music), Midas Dekkers (text), Olivia Ettema (illustrations), Arno van Berge Henegouwen (advice), Maarten van de Velde (photography)
Fabricators: Maqutos (interiors), Maquettebouw Bruns (props)

Blue Heron

Blue Heron was a coal camp, a small company-owned coal-mining town in the southeastern Kentucky hills not far from the Tennessee border. Run by the Stearns Company from 1938 to 1962, the Blue Heron mine processed its coal in the tipple which stood over the railroad siding, and virtually everything that was available to the people who lived in the camp was provided by the company: a church, a school, houses where the workers and their families lived, a company store, and eventually, after the miners struck briefly, a bathhouse. But in 1962 the coal ran out and the Stearns Company closed the mine. The town's inhabitants moved north to Lexington and its factories, or to other jobs in the local area, and the camp slowly decayed.

Hardly anything was left by the 1980s when the U.S. Army Corps of Engineers, who by then owned the land, decided to put up an interpretive center on the site. The tipple, where the coal was cleaned and loaded into railroad cars, was still there, but weathered and missing most of its siding. The bridge across the Big South Fork was there, too, but the houses, the church, and the school were all gone.

What the Corps handed designer Alex Cranstoun of DeMartin Marona Cranstoun Downes and his project

manager, Michael A. Hanke, were some previous master plans for the site, anthropology reports on the general area, and oral history tapes recorded by William Berge, a professor at Eastern Kentucky University. The Corps wanted something done with the site that would interpret its history to visitors. The site is part of the Big South Fork National River and Recreation Area, and Blue Heron is now the final stop on the area's scenic railway.

Dr. Berge turned out to be the key to the project. In working on an oral history of Eastern Kentucky, he had interviewed some former Blue Heron residents, and, even more important, he knew where they were presently living. Former residents like Norma Wright Trammel, Charles David, Christine Fradey, Betty Lou Davis West, Evelyn Ledbetter Coon, Simon Waters, and W. A. Pryor, among many others, had wonderful recollections of life at Blue Heron and they even had old snapshots. Both recollections and photos became an invaluable part of the exhibit.

Looking around Blue Heron in 1983, the designers found it ghostly. The dilapidated old tipple's framework was exposed behind missing siding and the old bridge was held from falling by a single pin. They were all

that was left and they conveyed a mood that the designers decided to try to keep. The community no longer existed. To recreate it would have been beyond the budget, and besides, no one remembered clearly how things looked. Everyone remembered architectural details differently. Three former residents, for instance, remembered the church steeple rising on the right side of the church roof; three people remembered it on the left, and three said it had been in the center.

Once the consultant engineers found they could shore up the bridge supports and that the tipple's framework was sound, the designers decided to let the structure's open framework represent the old tipple. By using just the framework, they reasoned, they could keep the town's ghostly feeling, suggesting what it had once been without re-creating it exactly. They could do the same for the coal camp's other structures—its houses, school, store, bathhouse, and church. Since they weren't sure what the structures had looked like, they would approximate their original framing, the way Robert Venturi of Venturi Rauch Scott Brown did with Benjamin Franklin's house in Philadelphia. It was as if they were setting out to sketch the old town

rather than produce an exact drawing.

They decided, too, that their interpretation should emphasize the people who had lived there. The question they wanted answered was: What was it like to live and work in this particular Appalachian coal-mining town in the years between 1938 and 1962? Coal-mining and its technical aspects would be a secondary part of the story.

To find out what the former residents had to say about life in Blue Heron, the designers sent William Berge out with his tape recorder to make additional tapes. The residents had a lot to say, and some of it was so good the designers wisely decided to let the voices of the former inhabitants become part of the exhibit. After editing the tapes to correspond to various aspects of Blue Heron life—bathhouse, woman's life, courtship and marriage, entertainment, school, church, the store, etc.—they played them in the corresponding structures. Project manager Michael Hanke had a loudspeaker fastened to each structure's roof framing, right beneath the peak of its galvanized steel roof. The designers transcribed the tapes onto video disks (for quality and long life, using only the audio portion) and ran underground cables to each structure from a

central control room in the visitors' center.

Used throughout the camp, the galvanized steel roofs became a visual element tying the skeletal community together. Dotted among the trees on the hillside, they are visible as visitors enter Blue Heron. The architect (Jack Ballard of Chrisman Miller Woodford) used steel decking for the roofs, the kind that concrete floors of high rise buildings are poured onto, because the decking is strong enough to span a large area with few supports. All the skeletal structures differ in size. Their floors are floating platforms

1. Site drawing.
2. Blue Heron coal tipple as it looked when mine was operating.
3. Coal tipple after 20 years of abandonment.
4. Coal tipple restored for exhibit with waiting railroad cars.

5. Open framework recreation of a Blue Heron home with material on Blue Heron family life. Each recreated structure has cut-out photo blowup of former resident.
6. Coal crossing bridge on way from mine to tipple.

7.

surrounded by green-painted metal railings, two feet within the green steel skeletal frames.

Also visible to arriving visitors are full-sized photo blowup cutouts of former residents, standing just inside the screen doors of each skeletal structure. These cutouts, like all site graphics, are fiberglass-embedded. Blown up from old snapshots, the photos are grainy and dissolve into an abstract as visitors approach them, a ghostly effect that Mike Hanke likes.

Besides the photo blowups and the sound of people's voices telling about life in Blue Heron, each structure has a pylon about 7' high and 3½' square with 3½'-high fiberglass panels that fold down to expose its glass-enclosed, internally lighted top section. Here on a back panel are snapshots, enlarged slightly, and text describing, in each particular structure, the appropriate aspect of Blue Heron life. These graphics are set in a 3"-square steel tube-stock frame, painted green to match the green steel frames of both the pylons and the town's skeletal structures. Inside the cases, in front of these rear panels, are artifacts that deal with each

theme, items like those used in Blue Heron from 1938 to 1962. To meet Park Service security rules, the artifacts couldn't be original, so the designers either re-created them or purchased similar items from local stores. When the front panel folds up for security, it displays on its outer surface the same graphics that are on the inside of the rear panel.

In some structures can be found, besides the pylons, bigger items that were once used there. For instance, in the church are pews, copied from the original Blue Heron pews which are now in another Appalachian church, while the steeple holds the Blue Heron bell, which visitors can ring. Next to the interpretive pylon is a button, like that found in all the other structures. Raised on a 4"-diameter square tube 30" off the floor, the button turns on the oral history disks. A voice on the audio disk says: "Sundays were real quiet there. It's hard to explain the quietness on Sunday. The church bell would ring. That was the noise."

In the school is a wood stove which visitors can observe while voices from the laser disk are heard saying in soft Kentucky accents: ". . . It was a little red school house. It had a big pot-bellied stove in the middle of the room. Had a water faucet outside the door. Not all schools in the area had that. In winter time it was very cold. One of the older boys was supposed to get there early and have the fire going before the rest of us came."

The Blue Heron mine entrance is still on the site and the designers wanted to use it,

8.

9.

10.

somehow, to let visitors enter the mine. "We wanted to convey the feeling of working in a coal mine" says Mike Hanke. But they found that bringing visitors 30' into the mine entrance would mean reinforcing the ceiling, which is only 40" high, at a cost of about $600,000. Instead, they took the suggestion of the engineers

(Ben Fister and Steve McKinley of GRW Engineers) to build a concrete extension with a 20'-wide opening in front of the mine entrance. They covered the concrete with earth and lined the interior with fiberglass coal. From the safety of this area, visitors could view a diorama installed in the real entrance, beneath the real coal ceiling, showing kneeling miners loading a coal car by hand.

Just outside the entrance extension, a refurbished mechanical loader that was actually used at Blue Heron stands as if waiting for the day in 1952 when it took over the job of loading from the miners.

Down by the railway tracks, beneath the truss roof of the newly constructed, open-sided Interpretive Center are three 7' pylons, each 4' square. Each carries four graphic panels explaining the workings of the mine, the tipple, the Stearns Company, and the town. Next to these pylons is a model of the tipple in a case 18' long, 2½' wide and about 2½' high, made of the same glass and green-painted steel as the cases in the site's other skeletal structures. Visitors can see through the case to the abstract reconstruction of the old tipple with its waiting Southern Railway cars. In front of the model on table-stands of the same green-painted steel are three 30" sloped graphic panels that explain how tipples worked and what the coal they processed looked like.

Also in the center is a 10'-by-10' model of the town as it looked in about 1950. On one wall is a 12' time line of the mine's history.

Visitors who come by train get off in front of the center by a 16'-long, 6'-high photo blowup of the Blue Heron miners in 1938, the year the mine opened. In front of the photo-mural are three lectern-style panels containing lists of the miners' names.

On the bridge is a blowup 18" wide and 2' tall of an old coal tram crossing the bridge. Also on the bridge is a section of track with a tram car on it and the original pin that held the bridge when reconstruction started—painted red, with an interpretive panel.

The project took six years on a budget of $14,000,000. Of that, the total exhibit budget was $850,000, not including the architectural structures, the mine entrance, or the cost of buying and putting in place the large artifacts such as tram and railroad cars.

Mike Hanke considers the U.S. Army Corps of Engineers, Nashville District, an ideal client. "Their attitude was: We trust your design concept and we want to do it right."

He has particular praise for the group of experts assembled to work on Blue Heron. They had the same attitude as the client and, for Hanke, part of the reward of the project was working with so many different disciplines: an oral historian, archeologist, mining engineer, anthropologist, landscape architect, civil and structural engineers, architect, and a writer/researcher. And, of course, working with and meeting the former residents of Blue Heron, who were excited by the interest being shown in their lives and work, was, Hanke says, "very satisfying."

11.

12.

7. Photo blowup of Blue Heron bridge on welcome sign.
8. Blue Heron interpretive reconstruction from the bridge.
9. Visitors arrive by train at the Blue Heron interpretive center.
10. Sixteen-foot-long photo mural of Blue Heron miners in 1938 is on wall where visitors get off train.
11. Recreation of Blue Heron church has original bell and pews.
12. Pylon with graphics in interpretive center.

Client: U.S. Army Corps of Engineers, Nashville District (Nashville, TN)
Design firm: DeMartin Marona Cranstoun & Downes, New York, NY
Designers: Alex Cranstoun (partner), Michael A. Hanke (project manager), Bruce Hanke (graphics)
Joint venture partners: Scruggs and Hammond (landscape architecture), John Scruggs, Joe Clark, Doug Maxon; GRW Engineers (civil and structural engineers), Ben Fister, Steve McKinley
Consultants: DMCD (interpretation and exhibit design); Nancy Campbell (research, writing, and conceptual design); Jack Ballard, Chrisman Miller Woodford (architecture); William Berge (oral history); Trebbe Johnson (audio production); Benita Howell (anthropology); Steve Gardner, Tri-State Engineering (mining); Jeffrey W. Gardner (archeology)
Fabricators: Exhibitgroup New York; Spectralite Ltd. (fiberglass embedments)

Japan: The Shaping of Daimyo Culture 1185-1868

Daimyos were lords in feudal Japan, just beneath shoguns. Shoguns would have the allegiance of several daimyos and, while Japan remained a feudal culture, daimyos controlled much of Japan. They were warriors. They spent a good deal of time gathering armies and fighting among themselves, and a strong martial tradition evolved, known as *bu*. According to this tradition, the ideal warrior was also a skilled civilian, a governmental administrator who could read and write and who had the cultural skills needed to mingle successfully with the courtly elite. It came to be expected that the daimyo, perhaps to mask his military power, would both nurture and participate in the peaceful arts of painting, calligraphy, ceramics—even fashion design—as well as dramatic and ceremonial arts. These peaceful arts were called *bun*. Their esthetics spilled over into the design of the accouterments of war, eventually involving a daimyo's weapons and battle dress. A warrior's sword, armor, saddles, sword mountings, etc., all became works of art. The ideal warrior embodied a balance of both *bu* and *bun*.

How some 450 Japanese works of art, once owned or produced by daimyos—mostly representing a dozen or so daimyo families—came to Washington, DC's National Gallery of Art is a story of insight, decisiveness, impeccable timing, and great good fortune.

Many of the items exhibited had never been out of Japan. The Japanese feel strongly

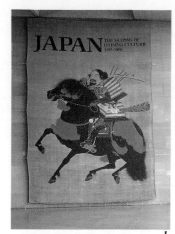

1.

about their artistic heritage and the government catalogs a good bit of this art, assigning rank according to a work's perceived importance. The most significant pieces carry a designation of "national treasures," next are "important cultural properties," and third are "important art objects." Among the works that traveled from Japan for a 3-month stay at the National Gallery were eight Japanese "national treasures" and almost 100 "important cultural properties."

At first, the Gallery was considering a Japanese show centered around one private collection, and a delegation went to Japan to see if anything else might be added for exhibition. Besides D. Dodge Thompson, head of the National Gallery's department of exhibition programs, the delegation included Gaillard Ravenel, chief, and Mark Leithauser, deputy chief, of its design and installation department, and Yoshiaki Shimizu, professor of art and archeology at Princeton University and guest curator of the exhibition. They traveled to

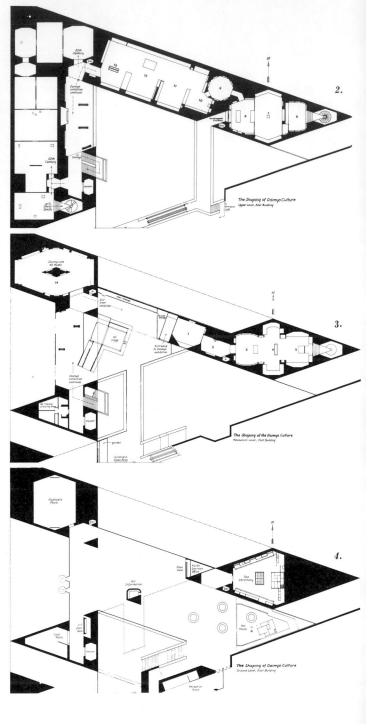

2.

3.

4.

5.

6.

7.

8.

Kyoto, visiting museums, shrines, palaces, tea houses and gardens, and they returned excited about the wealth of art available from the daimyo era. The delegation recommended to National Gallery director J. Carter Brown that, instead of displaying one collection, they should base an exhibit on the entire phenomenon of daimyo culture, drawing on a host of collections and sources.

While Yoshiaki Shimizu worked with scholars in Japan on a larger format, Carter Brown suggested that, besides *bu* and *bun*, they include examples of the dramatic and ceremonial arts that grew up in the daimyo culture and that the exhibit show at least photographs of daimyo castles and gardens. Accordingly, the National Gallery arranged for Japanese craftsmen, working on the ground floor of the Gallery's East Wing, to construct significant architectural and horticultural elements. These included a complete Japanese tea house and surrounding garden. The tea house was a separate room in which a regularly scheduled tea

ceremony took place and in which artifacts pertaining to the ceremony were displayed. In an open area on the mezzanine level adjacent to the exhibit entrance, the workers built a traditional Nō stage on which Nō plays were performed.

But the heart of the exhibit was the daimyo-era scrolls, paintings, ceramics, sculpture, armor, saddles, sliding doors, lacquer work, domestic textiles, Nō masks, musical instruments, robes, and tea utensils. In all, the exhibit took up 30,000 sq. ft. on three levels of the East Wing's space, making it the second largest exhibit—after "Treasure Houses of Britain"— ever staged at the National Gallery.

Visitors entered on the mezzanine level through a portal framed with large cedar beams. Over it, and over the Nō stage next to it, hung nine 24'-long, 4'-wide banners, each displaying the symbol of a daimyo family. The exhibit title was painted on the wall next to the entrance. What visitors saw first was a bonsai tree at the end of the entrance vestibule, borrowed for the exhibit from

9.

10.

11.

the National Arboretum. Off to the right was the exhibit's first room.

In this first room were a scroll of Minamoto Yoritomo, Japan's first shogun, and a polychromed wooden statue of him with inlaid crystal eyes. The scroll (a "national treasure") hung in a wall case lined with the grayish-tan linen that was hung behind all the scrolls and was framed, like all the exhibit cases, in antiqued cedar. Across the room, the statue sat on a cedar shelf in front of a backdrop of cedar boards fit together with chamfered edges. All the cedar here and throughout the show was antiqued to look old and weathered.

The designers kept the spaces neutral, painting the walls a light tan and covering the floor in a light tan nylon carpet. Against this, the reds, golds, and blacks of the armor, sculpture, scrolls, and screens stood out.

They also realized they had to use natural materials and textures—the cedar and linen and silks that the Japanese use—if they were to give the space a Japanese feeling. The amount of space was just as important as the materials, so each item was given plenty of room. Not only was there lots of space in each case or vitrine, but there was also enough space between items for visitors to stand back and view each item by itself. This generous space, the neutral color, and the simplicity of the exhibit design provided a sense of serenity.

Screens, scrolls, and swords mounted on silk-covered armatures went in wall cases.

Armor, porcelain, and lacquerwork were shown in free-standing vitrines with light bonnets that connected the vitrines to the ceiling, creating pillars within the space. The designers set all the porcelain flat on the vitrines' decks, the way it is displayed in Japan, rather than letting it float on armatures. Sculpture went behind waist-high railings of precisely joined cedar beams on antiqued cedar platforms in front of antique cedar planks.

Aluminum labels, painted to look like cedar (or whatever they were resting against) and silkscreened in large-type Garamond, lay flat throughout—on the sculpture platforms, within wall cases, and in vitrines.

Plexiglas central vitrines and Plexiglas wall cases made lighting difficult. To provide angles that would keep light from bouncing off the Plexiglas lighting, designer Gordon Anson retracked the entire light system. Then, except on the ceramics and the swords, he kept the light level low—5 to 10 foot-candles throughout—with the objects lighted only slightly more brightly than the ambient spaces.

Because the paintings, calligraphy, textiles, and lacquer items were so fragile, the National Gallery rotated them with similar items every four weeks during the exhibit's 12-week run.

This exchange meant, of course, that the exhibit design not only had to accommodate items of changing sizes, but had to make the changes physically possible. For instance, wall cases opened by the removal of almost invisible, tiny-headed

9. *Japanese tea house and garden built on lower level of exhibit by Japanese craftsmen.*
10. *Flasks crafted by daimyos in 17th century displayed in see-through case in front of wall case with robes.*
11. *Zen garden on mezzanine created for daimyo exhibit is now permanent part of East Wing of National Gallery.*

12.

screws. In the vitrines, a cedar slat that held one of the Plexiglas sheets in place came off and the sheet could be lifted out.

The designers' floor plan is ingenious in its configuration, taking visitors from narrow, relatively confined spaces into large, wonderfully varied, open spaces with long sight lines. At one point, visitors could look between two suits of armor in a vitrine to the 8' figure of a Buddha against horizontal antiqued cedar boards at the end of the room—a mixture of *bu* and *bun*. At another point, on the exhibit's upper level, a short corridor led visitors to an octagonal room whose tall wall cases held daimyo portraits, then out again in a different direction through another short passageway. The room served as what Ravenal calls a "knuckle," allowing him to change the exhibit's flow from west to northwest (following the building's configuration) without visitors realizing it.

In the final space of the exhibit's main galleries, a 90'-long wall vitrine held a screen undulating with intricately painted battle scenes. In front of it stood a 2½'-long toy boat, mounted on a wheeled board so it could be pulled. The boat had a gilded hull and polychromed topsides and on it sat the 2'-high polychromed wood figure of a child, Toyotomi Sutemaru, who died when he was two. The designers placed the boat and its cargo on a cedar pedestal, which they laid on a cedar platform surrounded by a waist-high cedar fence.

Visitors passed a wall case displaying large sliding-door panels painted with tigers (the same images used in the outside mural that announced the show), then moved into an elevator hall. Beyond that was an open area with wall-mounted blowups of daimyo castles and, on three free-standing monoliths, 12'-by-6', rear-lighted transparencies of Japanese gardens. Continuing on, down the stairs, viewers were back in the mezzanine space behind the Nō stage, where 4'-by-6' backlighted transparencies showed scenes from Nō performances. Beyond that was a separate room with daimyo and Nō masks. Except for the Nö artifacts, the exhibit was arranged chronologically and by category.

Also on the mezzanine level, designer Don Hand created a Zen garden of sand and rocks. Meant to complement the daimyo exhibit, it so suited the East Wing's I. M. Pei architecture that the National Gallery kept it as a permanent fixture.

The designers came to the Japanese daimyo exhibit from what Gil Ravenal refers to not at all unkindly as the "European clutter and formalities" of the "Treasure Houses of Britain." Dealing with the Japanese esthetic of the daimyo culture was, he says, "a wonderful change of pace."

Outside the building entrance, a 14th-century daimyo warrior in full armor on a black horse welcomed visitors. He was painted on a ceiling-high piece of fabric roped to the building.

In its 12 weeks, the exhibit drew more than a quarter-million persons, averaging 3383 a day.

14.

12. Daimyo armor in a room of swords on silk-draped stands in wall cases.
13. A toy boat in center of room with screens in wall cases.
14. Buddha figures on antiqued cedar platforms backed by walls of antiqued cedar boards.

13.

Client: National Gallery of Art (Washington, DC), J. Carter Brown, director. Exhibition organized by the National Gallery in collaboration with Japan's Agency for Cultural Affairs (Tokyo) and the Japan Foundation (Tokyo; New York, NY).
Sponsors: R. J. Reynolds Tobacco Co.; Yomiuri Shimbun; Nomura Securities Co. Ltd.; Tokyo Marine and Fire Insurance Co.; Nippon Life Insurance Co.; Matsushita Electric Industrial Corp.; Taisei Corp.; Shimizu Corp.; Ohbayashi Corp.; Japan Automobile Manufacturers Association, Inc.; Federation of Bankers Associations of Japan; Federal Council on the Arts and the Humanities (indemnity); Japan Air Lines (transportation)
Design firm: Design and Installation Department, National Gallery of Art
Designers: Gaillard F. Ravenel (chief), Mark Leithauser (deputy chief), Gordon Anson (lighting design, head of production), Barbara Keyes (graphic design), Chris Vogel (typesetting), Floyd Everly (head of exhibit construction)
Consultants: Yoshiaki Shimizu (guest curator)
Fabricator: Exhibits Shop, National Gallery of Art

Journey to the Heart of Matter

A good bit of the money for "Journey to the Heart of Matter," an exhibit of particle physics, came from TRIUMF, a Vancouver, British Columbia, physics research facility. The idea was to design an exhibit that would present the fundamentals of particle physics while showing some of the tools physicists use, and, of course—considering where the funds came from—the role research facilities play in physics research.

For eight months in 1990, the exhibit filled a 2200-sq.-ft. room at Science World British Columbia, a museum that opened in 1988 in a building left from the Vancouver world's fair, Expo '86.

Louise St. Pierre, who headed the exhibit design team, came to the museum as senior exhibit designer just four months before the exhibit opened. That gave her two months for design, working with a budget of $150,000 (Canadian). Before she joined the museum staff, the exhibit had been in rough planning for four months. St. Pierre, in effect, took a crash course in physics. Serving on a three-person team, along with a technical specialist from the museum's education department and an outside consultant physicist, she shared responsibility for the exhibit ideas and organization—then plunged into the design. The exhibit was to travel, so it had to be easily assembled and disassembled. But more important was translating the concept into design.

What TRIUMF and the museum wanted was an exhibit that treated the subject

sequentially, first giving visitors a basic understanding of particle physics, then introducing some of the research tools, and—finally—discussing specific research laboratories. So its framework became a linear path, and to make it palatable, the designers divided the information into small, easily absorbed packages.

Visitors entered the exhibit down a passageway lined with images painted on 12'-high canvases mounted on frames with a curved width of about 6'. These images of the Big Bang (the explosion that, according to current theory, started the formation of our universe), the cosmos, our galaxy, the earth, a city, and a house were intended to help visitors start thinking on an increasingly smaller scale, to recognize the vast difference in size between the universe and a human. This was all in preparation for thinking even smaller: down to molecules and atoms. In the background, digitally recorded voices discussed particle physics, asking questions about the origin of the universe, about the particles we are made of. At the image of the house, visitors passed through a keyhole-shaped portal into the main exhibit area. This section was laid out as two low-lit hallways, forming two sides of a V (see plan), lined with rows of glowing doors.

Behind these doors, which looked like ones in a 1930s office building, St. Pierre designed exhibits that explained some of the principles of physics quickly and simply. These were the kind of hallways off which private eyes Sam Spade or Mike Hammer

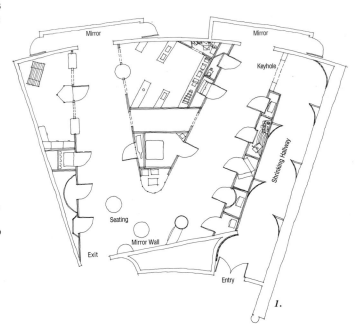

1.

2.

3.

4.

5.

6.

7.

8.

1. *Floor plan.*
2-4. *Early sketches of possible exhibit.*
5,6. *Views of left-hand hallway (see plan).*
7. *View of right-hand hallway.*
8. *Mezzotint image, taken from a photo which was screened and photocopied several times and mounted on Masonite, given a matte plastic protective lamination, and used as cabinet doors in one of exhibit rooms.*
9. *Typical translucent door panel lets light through but gives visitors only a hint of what is inside.*

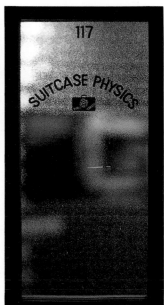

9.

might have had offices; the doors and the light which their frosted acrylic windows let into the dimly lighted halls were meant as metaphors for mystery and discovery. Indeed, behind one door was a mini-room 3' deep and 9' wide in which a bureau with drawers hanging open and contents spilled and an overturned chair hint at a crime. When visitors opened the door, they activated an old black-and-white TV, and a 1930s-type detective came on the screen describing the similarity between tracking a criminal and tracking a subatomic particle. "It's all in the clues left behind," he said. Another mini-room in the first hallway showed what he meant. It had a cloud chamber on a table; visitors standing over it could see the tracks of otherwise invisible particles.

On the hallway doors' frosted windows were room numbers and names, in hand-painted block letters, that hinted at the display within. For instance, behind the Universal Energy Management Company door was a mini-room with a diagram of the sun on a curved Sintra panel and a video monitor that explained how subatomic particles produce energy.

In the corridor area, at the point of the V made by the hallways, was a black wire grid and, behind that, a spark chamber, designed and built for the exhibit by TRIUMF personnel, on which particles that bombard earth from outer space show up.

In space opposite the spark chamber was a Sonotube monolith with a 48" TV screen embedded in it. The Sonotube was covered in Tarkett vinyl

flooring, which was also used to cover the round, hockey-puck-like seats accommodating about eight people in front of the screen. In the video program, a scientist explained the need for more advanced equipment to study particles.

The second hallway, the back side of the V, had rooms set up as physics laboratories and as an office to show how physicists work and the tools they use. These labs were not depicted exactly. For instance, the space behind one door revealed ordinary storage racks, painted with black-powder paint, holding 24"-wide Masonite panels laminated with black-and-white mezzotint images of electronic equipment. Facsimile acceleration tubes, one 3½' tall and the other 20" tall, had a beam, simulated in blue neon, passing through them. In one rack-mounted case is an interactive video game on which visitors could try to find the correct speed at which a particle beam would clear the accelerator.

It is not surprising that the displays that absorbed visitors the longest were those with interactive devices. There was an interactive computer that held information on ionization and on ways of tracking particles. Behind one door was a device on which visitors could test their reaction speed and compare it to the distance a subatomic particle would travel in the same time. They travel fast. "In the time it took me to react," says Louise St. Pierre, "the particle would have traveled to New York City and back."

In all, the exhibit had 18 displays. And probably the most

popular was not interactive. It was the door that opened onto a backlit, wall-mounted view of the galaxy. After a moment's pause came a flash and a loud explosive sound, and a video monitor mounted up near the ceiling at the back explained how scientists currently believe the universe began with a Big Bang. Science World edited these video sequences from an animated film donated by its author, Francis Aubry.

The Casebook jurors thought the doorways and period setting were a refreshing change from traditional exhibit design and they felt that kids would love

them. "Universal," they called the exhibit.

Louise St. Pierre quickly notes what pleased her most about the assignment: "It was watching people's reactions as they opened the doors." But she notes, too, that the doors created such a lure that visitors were not hesitating long at each one, but rather, rushing on to open another. Only if an open door revealed an interactive device would they pause for more than a few seconds. So, in most cases, attempts to get more than minimal information across were lost.

10.

JOURNEY
TO THE HEART OF
MATTER

11.

12.

13.

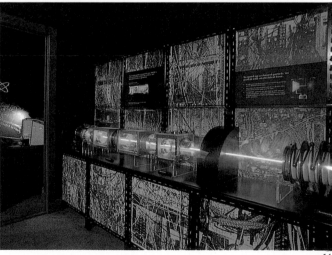

14.

This spark chamber is designed to fire only when a moving cosmic ray passes through, knocking electrons loose. When voltage is applied, the loose electrons carry the charge between the plates, creating a spark of miniature lightning. The sparks you see follow the path of the cosmic ray particle.

Spark Chamber designed, built and contributed by TRIUMF detector group members: Martin Salomon, Chris Stevens, Marielle Goyette, Robert Openshaw. (1989) Vancouver, B.C.

15.

10,12,13. Opening a door to an exhibit (Fig. 10) and two of the exhibits behind the doors.
11. Exhibit logo.
14. Model of particle accelerator in lab area.
15. Panel in spark chamber tracks path of cosmic rays.

Client: Science World British Columbia (Vancouver, BC)
Sponsors: TRIUMF; Ministry of Regional and Economic Development, Government of British Columbia; Science Culture Canada Program, Government of Canada
Design firm: Science World British Columbia
Designers: David Youngson (director of exhibits), Louise St. Pierre (senior exhibit designer), Celina Ducceschi (exhibit designer), Heather Griblin, Michael Rynar (graphic designers)
Consultants: Douglas S. Beder (physicist), David McGerrigle (technical specialist), Nancy Bryant (artist)
Fabricators: Warren Borden (director), Science World Fabrication Shop; B.S. Art

Reinstallation of the Permanent Collection, Walters Art Gallery

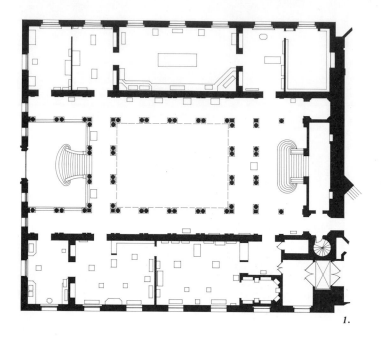

1.

Built in 1904 and turned over to the city of Baltimore in 1931, the original building of the Walters Art Gallery houses the collection of William and Henry Walters, father-and-son railroad tycoons and collectors. New York Times art critic John Russell called the Gallery "one of this country's great resources in the museum field." When Henry Walters made his gift to Baltimore, the collection had 22,000 items. It now has 30,000, with 2500 on permanent display in the newly refurbished original building.

In 1974, the Gallery added a wing which greatly increased its ability to display the collection. A physical link between the old building and the new wing was included in the 5-year process of renovation and reinstallation completed in 1989.

ElRoy Quenroe, whose firm, Quenroe Design Associates, did the exhibition design, spent a good part of the three years he devoted to the project helping curators William Johnston and Eric Zafran sort through the Gallery's collection of 14th-through 19th-century paintings and artifacts, paring it down to the 2500 they would display chronologically in the new installation. Then Quenroe, who has an architectural degree and specializes in architectural history, worked with the renovation architects, James R. Grieves Architects, to make sure the architectural renovation provided what Quenroe refers to as a "workable stage" for the exhibition design.

The architectural changes were actually few. One was the position of some of the doors between galleries. Many were off to one side so "you couldn't see the room properly as you entered," says Quenroe. "The sight lines were awkward and you had no sense of flow through the rooms." They moved these doors so visitors could see each gallery in its entirety as they entered and, more than that, could see on into the next gallery where an especially striking painting or piece of sculpture, displayed against that gallery's far wall, stood framed by the doorway. The designers also made the walls between galleries thicker. They had been no more than 6″ thick and gave visitors who passed through the doorways little sense of transition. Thickened to 1′ 6″, the walls provide a more solid feel and

allowed Quenroe to fit wall cases into them at the ends of some rooms. "Wall cases serve an architectural tradition," he points out, though it's not one the museum had previously utilized.

Wall color is an important part of the reinstallation, chosen both to complement the colors of the paintings set against them and to assure that transitions from one gallery to the next are not jarring. These colors, says Quenroe, "were subject to much historical and design debate." In the four upper-level painting galleries, the wall colors come mostly from brocaded cotton damask, specially woven for the Walters by Scalamandre, stretched tightly over frames hiding the uneven old walls. Gothic paintings and early Renaissance

2.

3.

4.

5.

6.

7.

works, for instance, many of which have gold on red backgrounds, now hang against bold red fabric-covered walls. These upper galleries have polished wood floors and skylights with newly added, sensor-activated louvers. Even so, spotlights still pinpoint each work, including the small bronze sculptures on wooden pedestals that serve as accent pieces.

Visitors enter the Walters up a grand staircase to a Great Courtyard originally designed to copy a courtyard in the Palazzo Balbi in Genoa. Among its marble column and arches, the Walters' marble sculptures show up against mustard/ champagne walls. Walters' director, Robert Bergman, matched the wall color with that in the Palazzo Balbi during a trip

to Genoa, and it brings out the gold tones of the marble. Quenroe designed sculpture pedestals of marbleized plywood, with details borrowed from the surrounding architecture.

In the seven carpeted, decorative art galleries opening off north of the Great Court, Quenroe used the Gallery's old metal-framed cases, with their turned hinges and clasps. He added shelves on brackets to hold mounts for jewelry and porcelains, and at the top of each vitrine he designed unobtrusive light-bonnets, detailed to look like the original cases, for low-voltage fixtures. Within these cases, he highlighted each piece of art, building mounts and covering them with rich maroon and blue moirés. He spent hours in the

Gallery's basement utilizing mockups that enabled curators to position each piece so that it worked with the ones around it. He found solutions in the same way for the cases in the travertine and wood-floored southern galleries (in all, seven decorative art galleries flank the court). But here, he used velvet over the mounts, in colors matching, or at least complementary to, those of the walls, to highlight and "help emphasize the crisp edges" of ivory sculpture, Limoges plaques, and Renaissance bronzes.

Bottoms of the cases now open to hold temperature- and humidity-controlling equipment. Some have touch-latch doors. Others open by lifting out the 4½"-wide slanted text panels (birch covered with dark brown

Formica) in their vitrines. Because the label boards are easily removed, they can be taken out and re-silkscreened if case contents are rearranged.

Quenroe's case designs picked up details of the Gallery's architecture, especially of the renovated wainscoting which runs throughout the building. He used walnut moldings and plywood with a walnut veneer.

Once decisions on which items would be in each case and how they would relate to each other were made, cases had to be arranged to relate to the ones nearby. Much of that work was done on the Gallery floor.

In only two instances did Quenroe depart from freestanding, furniture-like cases to hold decorative art. In the porcelain collection, he has

8.

9.

a built-in wall case, and in a library-like room filled with jewelry by Tiffany and eggs by Fabergé, there is a whole wall of built-in cases.

For a typeface, the designers specified New Baskerville, which the Gallery had used before. They screened texts on clear acrylic wall plaques, which were then back-painted with the color of the wall behind them.

Quenroe stresses the care he took to let nothing in the exhibit design intrude on the art, and more than that, to make sure each piece is highlighted. What has given him most pleasure is hearing regular Walters visitors say they have never seen some of the objects before, even though they were on display in the old installation. Curators who have studied particular objects for years," says

Quenroe," report that they now notice new things about them." Critic John Russell wrote: "There is no museum in the country that could not learn something from what has been done under Robert Bergman's direction. What has resulted is as much a rebirth as a rehabilitation."

6-9. The new exhibition installation displays fewer pieces, giving each ample space and usually its own light and setting.
10,11. Small pieces in vitrines are individually mounted so that each stands out from the others.

10.

11.

Client: Walters Art Gallery (Baltimore, MD)
Sponsors: City of Baltimore; numerous corporations and individuals (list available from Gallery)
Design firm: Quenroe Design Associates, Baltimore, MD, and Boulder, CO; ElRoy Quenroe, principal
Consultants: George Sexton Associates (lighting); James R. Grieves Architects (building renovation)
Fabricators: Exhibits Unlimited; John Klink, head of exhibitions installation staff, Walters Art Gallery

Familia Y Fe

Hispanic Heritage Wing
Museum of International Folk Art

2.

Photos by Michel Monteaux

1.

3.

The Casebook jurors called "Familia Y Fe" (Family and Faith) "beautiful," and there is little question that the exhibit setting is as beautiful and as carefully detailed as the artifacts exhibited. The exhibit is a permanent installation in the Hispanic Heritage Wing of New Mexico's International Folk Art Museum in Santa Fe, which is a unit of the Museum of New Mexico.

The jurors also praised the mood the exhibit evokes, the feeling of the Southwest's Hispanic culture which emerges from the installation's depiction of the area's art, architecture, crafts, and religion. This mood was what exhibition designer Julie Bennett worked hard to achieve. A staff designer with the Exhibitions Unit of the Museum of New Mexico, Bennett joined the project a year and a half before the exhibit opened. It's pre-design planning had been going on for almost three years before that.

Bennett and the International Folk Art Museum staff (including a visiting curator) ended up displaying some 350 items from the folk art collections, about one-tenth of what the museum has in its

archives. They designed into the 4000-sq.-ft. exhibit space a changing gallery which every six months will open a temporary exhibit incorporating some of the artifacts still in storage.

Visitors enter the Historic Heritage Wing from either the Girard Wing, which houses the breathtaking folk art collection bequeathed to the museum by Alexander Girard, or from the Bartlet Wing. Entrance is into what the designers call a courtyard, an introductory area which immediately immerses visitors in the materials, colors, architectural details, sounds, and especially the light of the Southwest. The bright New Mexico light pours into the space through a massive, peaked, wood-mullioned skylight, designed and installed especially for this exhibit.

Marching along the wall between the two entrances are four wooden-framed maps, each 40″ by 46″, carrying 8″-by-12″ texts in similar blond wood

frames mounted on the left-hand vertical side of each map frame. On the maps are routes followed by early explorers and settlers of the New Mexico territory.

Three couches covered in a black-and-white fabric woven locally in traditional patterns form a U-shape in front of a 4′-by-10′ model of an 1800s Hispanic village. Next to the model and the couches is a re-creation of the balustrade of a traditional porch, and on the porch—next to a traditional window deeply inset into the wall, the way it would be in the wall of an adobe house—is a row of hanging *ristras*, the traditional strings of red peppers. Also in the introductory courtyard is a 5′-by-10′ sepia-toned photo blowup of an Hispanic family. The courtyard's floor is of red tiles made from a local clay.

All the courtyard's artifacts—*ristras*, maps, tiles, fabrics—are meant as props for an audiotape in Spanish of *cuentos* (tales) of

the region's settlement, exploration, and conquest. Visitors can sit on the couches and listen to the tape, or portions of it (it runs three hours), and even if they do not pause, or even if they do not understand Spanish, the sound of spoken Spanish in the background helps set the mood of the exhibit.

Opposite the village model, visitors pass through wooden doors, specially commissioned from a local craftsman, that stand open like outstretched welcoming arms. Above the door is the exhibit title "Familia Y Fe" in script laser-cut from Mild Steel. "The designer who drew up a preliminary design to present for grants scratched a title on the plan in pencil," says Julie Bennett. "We blew this up and used it."

Inside the door, beyond the sound and bright outside light of the courtyard, is the exhibit's 2200-sq.-ft. main gallery. Its first section is devoted to Faith, the *Fe* of the exhibit title. A complete altar stands in a chapel-alcove to the right. Wooden figures of saints look out over it from wall niches and a brightly painted traditional wooden altar rail stands in front

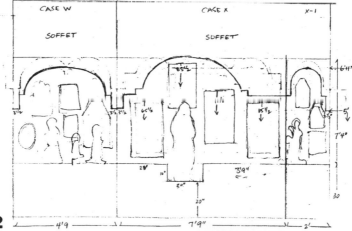

5.

6.

7.

8.

**FAITH:
A SOURCE OF UNITY**

Until the mid-1800s Hispanic New Mexicans had only one religion: Roman Catholicism. In contrast to the many, often conflicting, sects of eastern America and northern Europe, almost everyone in New Mexico subscribed to the tenets of the one religion, often with a deep sense of faith. Religion thus provided a source of unity that transcended social differences and gave order to community, family and individual life.

9.

of it. The chapel's ceiling of log beams, held by corbels from the museum's collection, and floor of hard-packed mud are traditional, too.

Lighting comes from spots ceiling-mounted behind a lip at the front edge of the ceiling above the altar. Like all of the exhibit's lighting, these spots are the work of Ian Rosenkranz, a Santa Fe theatrical lighting designer.

Several of the designers working on the exhibit had backgrounds in theater design. Bennett, for instance, did a stint as a set designer for the Santa Fe Opera before joining the museum. "A vital part of the exhibit's success," she says, "derived from what the theater-oriented designers brought to the project."

Opposite the altar are wall cases which hold *retablos*, paintings of saints, usually on wood, often used as altar pieces, and three-dimensional wooden saints, called *bultos*, the work of craftsmen, known in the Southwest as *santos*. The exhibit displays the work of seven different *santos*.

A 40"-high dado runs along the walls in the Fe section, through the altar space and just beneath the cases. Here, it is painted in yellow clay, contrasting with the white plaster walls above it. Bennett used the dado, in wood or clayslip (clay mixed with water and glue), *bancos* (platforms on which she set items for display), wood and brass lintels, and horizontal antiqued lines in the text panels as "a horizontal motif" to move visitors through the gallery. She felt the exhibit design needed some sort of horizontal constant because its

1. *Title panel with backlit arch.*
2. *Floor plan.*
3. *Straw-appliquéd crosses in wall case with frame designed in territorial style.*
4. *Case sketch.*
5. *Entrance courtyard with benches, and ristras (strings of red peppers) behind porch balustrades next to traditional deep-set window.*
6. *Overhead zaguan (covered vestibule) marks transition between exhibition sections.*
7. *Recreation of New Mexican room from the 1860s. Touch-screen video at left is keyed to objects displayed.*
8. *View through transition vestibule into exhibit's Family section.*
9. *Graphic panel with starburst graphic screened above it. Drop capital is from old Hispanic text.*

10.

11.

vertical elements changed height continuously.

Thus, Bennett designed short *zaguans* (vestibules) as transitions from one exhibit section to the next, with ceilings made of narrow (2″-to-3″-thick) finished logs laid across larger, traditional log beams. Lights above these ceilings shine through the spaces between the branches, throwing patterns on the floor that further define the transitions. The ceilings of the *zaguans* are only 8′ above the floor while the gallery ceiling is 14′ high.

Though she disliked doing it, Bennett mounted all the artifacts in the next section, Styles and Sources, in glass cases. She would have preferred having them in the open, but there was not enough space to let graphic rails offer security. As it was, she had to arrange the cases to create even more space, forming alcoves by setting cases at right angles to the walls. Shelves in the cases, varying from 5″ to 20″ in depth, serve here as the horizontal line, running through the space either 20″ or 30″ off the floor. The Styles and Sources section continues the theme of Faith, presenting more of its art—*bultos* and *retablos*—and history.

Looking toward security, the designers specified ½″-thick glass for the cases, then found when it came that its thickness gave it a green tint. To make it colorless, they placed gels in various warm colors on the clear acrylic light soffits of the cases and played spots down through them onto the glass. The glass fronts of the wall cases are 7′ 10″ high. All have glass fronts that open on pivot hinges at the top and bottom and close with a lock in the upper rail.

To position each artifact in its case, Bennett used templates cut from kraft paper to match the piece's profile. To each template, she glued a Xerox copy of a Polaroid photo of the item. After adjusting the templates in each case, the designers tacked them down and the preparators, who had a Xerox version of each item along with its mounting instructions, drilled right through the templates to make sure each item was exactly placed.

Through another vestibule is the exhibit's Family section. Here is a massive loom on a mud-plastered 9"-high platform along one wall. Next to it, on a 24"-high platform, also mud-plastered, are examples of 18th-century furniture. Behind them, against the wall, fabrics hang on frames between mud-plastered buttresses of the type added to sagging adobe structures. The feeling the designers sought was of a workplace in a New Mexico courtyard. In front of the platform, and 6" lower, is a 16'-by-18"-wide case holding agricultural and woodworking tools. Labels were put on an angled panel between the case and the platform above.

Across from the platform is a 14'-by-7' period reproduction of a New Mexican room from the 1860s. And just in front of that is a video stand and a wall-mounted slave monitor. Using the touch-sensitive screen on the 12" stand-mounted unit, visitors can, for instance, touch a rug and call up a video

segment on weaving. And they can do the same to find out how most of the other tools in the case across the room were used. The videotape is bilingual, and at a touch of the screen the narration shifts instantaneously from one language to the other.

The final section is Agents of Change, devoted to artifacts of the 20th century when the railroad reached the territory, when power tools replaced hand tools and plaster replaced mud. Inset into a wall here are a pair of 3'-high shutters, looking as if they have just been locked for the night. The woodwork has moldings and is smoothly finished in contrast to the rough-hewn look of the wood throughout the rest of the exhibit. In a wall case, against embossed wallpaper made in England, are several artifacts of tin that began to replace wood.

Visitors leave the artificially lighted earth tones of the main exhibit and step out into a *mirador*, a window-walled room looking out to views of the Jiminez mountains. On a back mud-plaster wall, agricultural implements are bolted to 6'-high plywood panels. This wall also displays 11"-by-14" photo blowups of farmers, of horses threshing, of people shucking corn. Eventually, the museum hopes to have an apple orchard outside the *mirador's* windows. A bench is already in place inside where people can sit and look at the view. But people rarely sit there. "We thought of putting up a 'Please Sit' sign," says Bennett. Where they do sit, of course, is on the low case of old tools across from the video monitors in the gallery's Family section.

Certain details make this

exhibit unusual: the use of embossed wallpaper and deep red or gold colored Ultrasuede as backdrops in the cases, for instance, and antiqued, rough-hewn wood and white pine flooring to match the feeling of the artifacts. Texts have decorative graphic elements screened above them, a starburst pattern or an arch, graphics taken from the exhibit's *retablos*. Bennett chose Palatino typeface because she wanted a serif face that was available on both the museum's typesetter and vinyl lettering machine. To this she added drop capitals taken from script found in Hispanic texts in the museum's archives.

Perhaps the ultimate detail was the gold plating given the security screws that hold a case of gold jewelry. "I couldn't find brass," says Bennett in an explanation that probably says more about the exhibit's budget than about Santa Fe hardware stores. In fact, this is one of the few exhibits where the budget ($1,250,000) allowed the designers to do almost everything they wanted.

12.

13.

10. Case detail. Styles section case has arch reliefs on wall and subsection labels on glass keyed to Dynamart labels inside.
11. Family crafts section with furniture, rugs, a loom, and, in lower case, ironwork items.
12. View through territorial-style doorway to Agents of Change section.
13. Looking across relief model of an 1800s New Mexican village through the open doors of the exhibit entrance.

Client: Museum of International Folk Art, a unit of the Museum of New Mexico (Santa Fe, NM)
Sponsors: New Mexico State Legislature, National Endowment for the Humanities, National Endowment for the Arts, International Folk Art Foundation
Design firm: Exhibitions Unit, Museum of New Mexico
Designers: Julie Bennett (exhibit design), Nancy Allen (assistant designer), Ian Rosenkranz (lighting), Janet Persons, Daniel Martinez, Helen McCarty, Marmika (graphics), Phil Nakamura, J. Pearson (preparation)
Consultants: Blair Clark (photography), Richard Connerty (plaster), Felipe Ortega (clayslips), Lynn Osborne (scenic painting), Michael Motley, Michael Picón (auxiliary graphics), Sign Associates (map production), Sonitrol, Inc. (security), Richard Skinner (lighting), Robert Pepper (special cabinetry), Rogow and Bernstein (design), Mazria Associates (architectural renovations)
Fabricators: Thayer Carter (lead carpenter and construction design), Charles Sloan (on-site fabrication), Ron Anaya, Peter Oppenheimer (carpenters)

The Mandell Futures Center

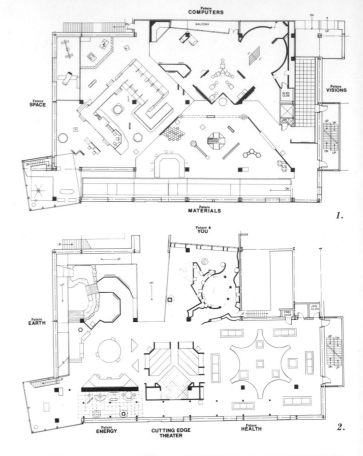

1.

"The assignment," says Sanderson Caesar, director of design at Philadelphia's Franklin Institute Science Museum, was "to design eight exhibits that would showcase future science and technology and explore the ramifications these would have on our lives." The result is the Mandell Futures Center, which adds 20,000 sq. ft. of exhibits on two levels. Originally built in 1930 in an L configuration, the institute has long had science exhibits and a planetarium. The building addition that houses the Futures Center fills in much of the space within the L, turning it into more of a U, and adds, besides the Futures exhibits, a 2-story atrium which connects the new addition, the old building, and a 350-seat Omnivision Theater. In all, the addition and the new theater with its 4-story screen roughly double the Franklin Museum's space.

The Futures exhibits were to do three things:

1. Showcase present-day science that will almost certainly underlie future technology.

2. Present technologies currently being worked on in research labs that may become part of our lives in five or 10 years.

3. Give a glimpse or two of technologies (existing or anticipated) that may affect the way humans live in the distant future.

Suggestions for the philosophical and actual content came from a museum advisory committee that included, besides exhibit designer Sanderson Caesar, the museum's chairman, Charles Andes; its president, Joel

Bloom; the senior director of exhibits, William H. Booth; the chairman of the building and grounds committee, Burdell Buckley; and the architect, Robert Geddes, of Geddes Brecher Qualls Cunningham. They and other committee members submitted their incipient concept to an advisory group of futurists, scientists (including at least one Nobel laureate), and computer experts.

What they decided on was a smorgasbord of eight exhibits that would address the future of both emerging and industrialized societies, arranged more or less randomly, so visitors would move through them freely, seeking out whatever seemed of individual interest.

Each of the eight explores a different topic. These, and the space they occupy, are: Future Visions, 1250 sq. ft.; Future Computers, 3000 sq. ft.; Future Space, 3600 sq. ft.; Future Materials, 2000 sq. ft.; Future Earth, 3500 sq. ft.; Future Energy, 1600 sq. ft.; Future Health, 3500 sq. ft.; Future and You (including Careers Center), 1275 sq. ft.

The designers realized that every hour the Tuttleman Omniverse Theater would disgorge 350 viewers. Seventy-five of these, the designers reasoned, would come directly to the Futures Center. But the designers figured that the random flow pattern (which the Franklin Museum has always used) would quickly scatter visitors through the Futures Center's 20,000 sq. ft. "I've seen kids on a playground do the same thing they do here at the Center," says Sandy

2.

3.

4.

1. Floor plan, upper level.
2. Floor plan, lower level.
3,4. Model Future and You section.
5. Assembly plan for column in Future and You section.
6. Futures Center second level seen from Franklin Museum central courtyard. Neon outlined mechanical hand and human hand reach for each other.
7. In Future and You section, screens illustrate possible future of television. Graphic panels are attached to wall with giant pushpin-headed fasteners.
8. Ten-foot-diameter fiberglass globe has fiber optic light points that wink on to show human population gains through the centuries.
9. Giant 30' fiberglass cell arches overhead in the Future Health section.
10. In Future Vision section, tunnel of graphics and reflective glass projects images related to the Center.
11. Exhibit space flows into the Future Computers section.

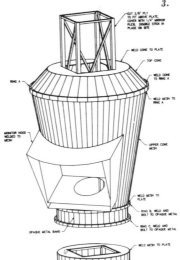

5.

6.

7.

8.

9.

10.

11.

Caesar. "They rush to the thing they like best, then they rush to the thing they like second best while another group comes to the first thing."

Most visitors enter on the first level, between Future Vision and Future Earth. As they approach the new wing from the atrium, they see two giant neon arms and hands against the glass walls that separate the futures exhibits from the atrium. "These are a play on Michelangelo's Sistine ceiling," says Caesar. "Instead of the hand of God reaching for the hand of man, we have the hand of man reaching for a robotic hand."

Inside, the exhibits are laid out according to the original precepts. The designers positioned individual exhibits as islands floating in the space, and for the most part they kept the space open rather than dividing it into rooms or galleries. Walls built to hold graphics and to direct flow are only 8′ high, more like partitions than walls. On each level, for roughly each 10,000 sq. ft. of space, are two large central displays. The Franklin Museum designers call these displays "magnets," in much the same way shopping center developers call the department stores at the ends of malls "anchors." On the first level, one magnet is a 30′-by-30′ fiberglass model of a human immune cell in the Future Health area. The other is a 10′-diameter fiberglass globe in Future Earth.

The cell arches overhead like a giant parachute so visitors can walk beneath it, and hanging from the ceiling are Plexiglas reproductions of organelles (parts of the cell that act like organs). All this is illuminated by three different kinds of lights hanging from six light bars: lamps with colored gels, fresnel lens lamps, and lamps with rotary disks filled with liquids producing a bubble-like effect that makes the cell seem alive.

The 10′ globe in the Future Earth area has continents formed from airbrushed auto-body putty. Within the continents are 10,000 fiber optic light points, each representing 1.2 million human beings. These wink on in sequences representing 30-year intervals from 1780 to 2050, showing where humans lived (or will live) and in what concentrations. A wall-mounted LCD display near the globe gives the earth's human population second by second. Silkscreened on the wall beneath the display are instructions asking visitors to count to five. In that time, says the caption, the world population has increased by 12. Six months after the Futures Center opened, the world population, according to the display, was 5.357 billion. A caption points out that at current rates of growth, that figure will double in the next century.

Also in the Future Earth area is what arguably could be called another magnet, a self-contained waterfall descending 12′ into a pool surrounded by a tropical rainforest fabricated from silk, fiberglass, and real Spanish moss. Triangular-shaped kiosks hold photos and text. In Future Earth, and throughout the Futures Center, are a host of interactive video programs. In Future Earth, visitors touch video screens to see programs on the greenhouse effect, ozone depletion, acid rain, and tropical deforestation. There are enough video devices to make their sound levels a potential source of audio clutter. "We adjust the audio levels according to the size of the crowds," says Sandy Caesar. Also, in displays which have ambient sound, the designers used devices to create sound puddles. One is a parabolic dish, a saucer 30″ across and 6″ deep. "We aimed the speaker at the dish and the dish throws the sound to the floor. We also used Sonotubes 3½′ long and about 1′ in diameter with a speaker inside, aimed down. And we are sure to have carpet beneath these devices to catch the sound." They also used telephone receivers wherever possible and musical overrides.

Visitors, as noted, enter the Futures Center between Future Earth and Future Vision. If they turn left, they enter Future Vision, an area conceived as an introduction. In it, outside designer Carlos Ramirez covered walls and ceiling with dark, tempered reflective glass that makes a kaleidoscope of suspended color photo blowups, reinforcing major themes of the Center. Images display the relationships between people of all ages and races and their interplay with natural and man-made environments and with technology. In the background, a soundtrack plays a mix of voices of people talking about their hopes and fears, about life in the coming century—along with sounds of nature and New Age music.

The designers tried to give the exhibit a look that might

12.

13.

12. Laboratory equipment in Future Materials section.
13. Unisystem, a computer system that guides visitors around the Futures Center.
14. Rain forest segment is part of Future Earth.
15. Space transport and space station module are also part of Future Earth.
16,17. Future Computers section.
18. Future fashion in Future and You section.
19. Wall graphics link health and exercise in Future Health section.

14.

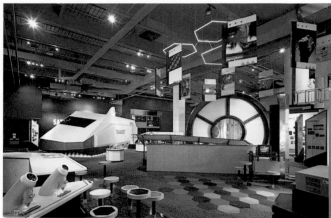

15.

16.

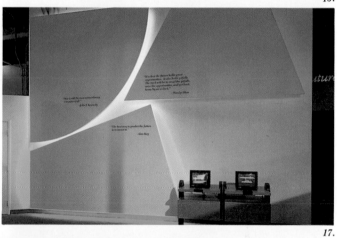

17.

18.

19.

subliminally speak of the future. And although this may seem a task almost impossible to fulfill without producing a set that looks as if it came from a *Star Trek* movie, the curved shapes of the exhibit devices and the gloss of its metals and plastics do nudge a visitor's perception toward the future.

Outside design firms designed four of the Futures Center's exhibits, and the Franklin Museum exhibition design staff designed the other four. Designers of the exhibits on each floor met to select a common ceiling color and to coordinate carpet selection, but otherwise they selected their own exhibit colors. Of course, wall colors had to flow smoothly from one exhibit to another. The Franklin Museum design staff worked out guidelines for typefaces (Univers, Futura, Garamond, Caledonia, Palatino) and sizes. Graphics and type on many of the cases are silkscreened directly to the wall. "We find that if the graphics are vertical, we don't have to protect them," says Caesar. "If they're horizontal, we do have to protect them."

On the upper level, the two magnet displays are a 40′-by-15′ model segment of the proposed U.S. space station and a 36′ mock-up of the space transport's nose section. Visitors sitting at one of three flight simulators in the transport can follow NASA images and cooperate with other visitors at ground control consoles (10′ away) to assemble a space station. Made of aluminum, steel, Formica, and Sintra, the space station has 10 work-station bays lining its interior walls. Each bay holds a different

interactive device, demonstrating an aspect of life in space, e.g., sleeping, exercise, meals.

What do visitors like best at the Futures Center? A few examples:

● "See Yourself Age" in the Future Health exhibit. A computer takes your video image, freezes it, then pinpoints future sagging at some eight points. All this happens on a 24″-screen with a seat in front of it for one person and plenty of room for others to stand and watch.

● Future Computers has a jamming room where visitors can make music on electronic instruments, such as a drum-controller and a trackball keyboard.

● On a fluid dynamics device in the Future Earth exhibit, visitors spin a 4″-deep, 3′-diameter cylindrical chamber, allowing reflective crystals to set up swirls and eddies in a deep turquoise fluid. These swirls behave much like clouds in the atmosphere.

● A 6′-tall Neuron sculpture in the Future Health exhibit uses fiber optics and luminous plasma balls to represent electrochemical impulses in the brain. Colored lights cascade through the device as visitors manipulate it with joysticks. It shows how the human brain handles whatever is fed into it.

The Futures Center also has an area of its Future and You section (the work of another outside design firm, Design, Etc., Inc.) devoted to future career choices. Here, against wall graphics made up of help-wanted ads, are touch-sensitive video screens on which visitors can call up descriptions of jobs

that will be available in the future.

An interactive computerized information system called Unisystem, designed (on a 5-year grant) by a special Franklin Institute design team, has 42 terminals throughout the museum. The system uses 42 personal computers and six mini-computers. Visitors can use Unisystem to design a museum visit that investigates a special scientific theme, or to get a print-out of a scientific bibliography, or even to read a profile of a scientist in the news. It will answer the most frequently asked question: "Where's the bathroom?"

Exhibit design for the Futures Center took three years on an overall budget of $4.5 million.

20.

20. Cover of "Experience Tomorrow" folder from the Mandell Futures Center.

Client: The Franklin Institute Science Museum (Philadelphia, PA)
Sponsors: *Future Health:* Smith Kline Beecham Foundation, Independence Blue Cross, Merck Co. Foundation, Sterling Drug, Inc., Rorer Group, Inc., U.S. Health Care, Inc., Mediq, Inc., Dr. Arnold T. Berman; *Future Space:* The Boeing Co., G.E. AstroSpace Division; *Future Computers:* IBM Corp., SEI Corp., Commodore Business Machines, UNISYS Corp.; *Future Earth:* ARCO Chemical Co., Waste Management of North America, Inc., Scott Paper Co. Foundation, Jesse R. Wike Charitable Trust, Betz Laboratories, Inc.; *Future Energy:* Sun Co., Certainteed Corp.; *Future Materials:* Du Pont; *Future Visions:* Cigna Foundation, CMS Corp.; *Future and You:* Safeguard Scientifics, Inc.; *Future Careers:* Bell of Pennsylvania
Design firm: Franklin Institute Science Museum Design Dept.
Designers: Sanderson Caesar (director); Donna Claiborne (assistant director); Ted Anderson, Dana Bertles, Karyn Kahn, Barbara Punt (exhibit designers); Julie Fabi (senior graphic designer); Susan Capezzone, Carol Carr, Scott Hyman, Maureen Kelly, Diane Quinto, Randy Strader (graphic designers); Barbara Biscardi, Nicole Hagedorn, Terri Mallon, Raymond Rorke, Nancy Rosenberg, Lisa Troncelliti (graphic assistants)
Consultant designers: Don Campbell, Ricardo Martin, Design, Etc., Inc.; Shab Levy, Gary Larsen, Levy Design, Inc.; Don Burns, Matt Kasar, Museum Design Resources; Carlos Ramirez, Carlos Ramirez, Inc.; Charles Capaldi, Robert Geddes, Michael Kihn, James Rowe, Geddes Brecher Qualls Cunningham; Ken Getz, Eric Getz, Ken Getz Design; Tony Junker, Joseph Nicholson, Ueland and Junker Architects
Fabricators: R.H. Guest, Inc., The Magic Lantern, Showtime Exhibit Builders, City Sign Co., Kleinman Cabinet Co., General Engineering, Quinlan Scenic Studios, Holographics North, Monadnock Media, Inc., Four Color Lab, Levy Design, Inc., Lynch Exhibits, Falk Special Effects Corp., Paramount Industries, Inc., Sierra Productions, Art Guild, John Spillane Co., The New Curiosity Shop, Keystone Scientific Co., Rolle, Gander and Showalter, Inc., Kenneth Pfaltzgraff

Esprit Shoe and Accessories Showroom New York

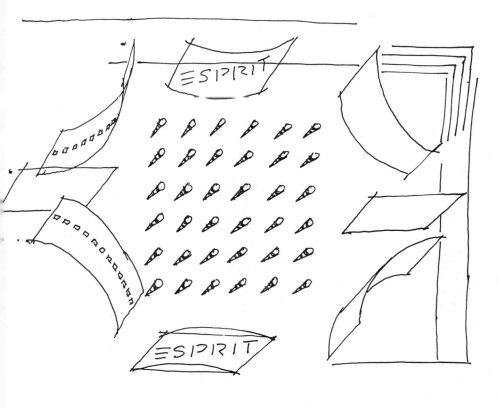

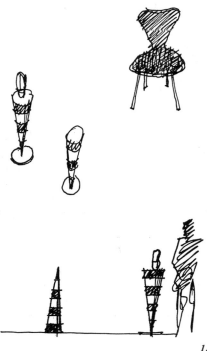

1. Isometric drawing of exhibit space and preliminary design sketches.

1.

If the 25 black-and-white striped cones standing at attention in this temporary showroom in New York City's Rockefeller Center are ice cream cones, then the shoes, belts, and handbags they hold for review are the ice cream, and that is sort of what the designers had in mind. They wanted these items, made by Esprit, the San Francisco clothing company, to look delectable if not edible to professional buyers. But, even more important, the designers, from Vanderbyl Design, saw the cones as the solution to a very real problem: how to make a product line of small objects stand out in a relatively vast

space (4500 sq. ft. beneath a ceiling as high as 18′).

By partitioning off space in each of the area's corners, the designers created rooms with chairs, desks, and shelves where salesmen could sit with buyers and still watch the showroom floor. Aluminum panels (10′ by 4′) were bolted together to form a curved façade for each corner sales space. Into each panel were cut four 8″-square windows, positioned at eye level of a seated salesman. So an eight-panel partition would have 32 windows through which salesmen could monitor floor traffic.

Visitors entered the space

past a sales desk placed in a public elevator hall which the designers draped in black. Behind the reception desk, a pyramid of brightly colored Esprit show boxes served as a logo to guide buyers to the showroom. Inside the door, a corrugated aluminum wall slanted into the room so that entering visitors would stand directly in front of the platoon of black-and-white striped cones. At the back of the room, the name Esprit, in open 15″-high letters, was cut across six aluminum panels. Behind each letter, the designers set up six high-intensity lamps. Michael Vanderbyl, whose firm has done a number of showrooms for

Esprit, calls the effect "slightly theatrical and in keeping with the space's hyper-tech ambience."

The designers ingeniously mounted shoes to pedestals in whimsical attitudes which they felt were in keeping with the client's high-spirited image. They fitted a wooden block into the toes of the shoes, then drilled through the toe and screwed a headless bolt both to the shoe and to the 11″-wide pedestal top. Belts were fastened to armatures the same width as the belts and painted the same color. Each pedestal was bolted to 16″-diameter bases of ¼″ steel.

Vanderbyl had used rubber

floor matting in the previous showroom he designed for Esprit, and he wanted something different for this one. His search turned up black Astroturf, which came in 5′-widths with rubber edges. The edges were cut off and the Astroturf rolled out with carpet holders to keep it in place.

The room's walls were clad with 12′-high aluminum panels and, in the salesmen's spaces, curving 1′-wide shelves were fastened to aluminum panels with aircraft cable. The cable ran from the upper wall fastening over the edge of the shelves and back to the lower wall fastening. "It took a while to get the proper tension on the cables," says Vanderbyl. Cables stretching from floor to ceiling held the 16′ horizontal curve of the aluminum salesmen's desks. Each salesmen's room also had a few ICF chairs (designed by Philippe Stark) with black rubber seats stretched tightly across black steel tubular frames.

The Vanderbyl designers' original budget was $60,000, but there was some give and take in it, and the showroom, whose components were manufactured in San Francisco and shipped to New York, came in for $18 per square foot.

Doug Tompkins, head of Esprit, liked the showroom so well that he had it disassembled when the show was over and shipped back to San Francisco to be set up in the company headquarters.

Says Vanderbyl of his client: "He wants your fresh input. He just expects you to do a better job than you've ever done before, and he leaves you alone to do it."

3.

2.

4.

5.

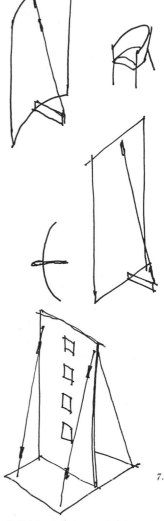

7.

6.

2. Headless bolts fasten pedestal to wooden block.
3. Square-cut perforations in aluminum partitions let sales staff see into showroom.
4. Curving aluminum counter and shelves suspended by aircraft cable. ICF chairs are by Philippe Stark.
5. Esprit logo cut in aluminum panels leads into showroom.
6. Banded conical supports line up on black Astroturf carpet.
7,8. Preliminary design sketches.

Client: Esprit Corp. (San Francisco, CA)
Design firm: Vanderbyl Design, San Francisco, CA
Designers: Michael Vanderbyl (designer), Peter Fishel (project manager)
Consultants: Bruce and Bruce Scenery, Thomas Swan Sign Co.
Fabricator: Thomas Swan Sign Co.

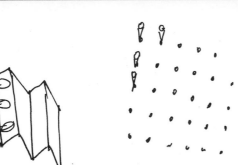

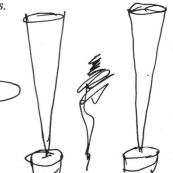

8.

"Traveling the Pacific" is a departure from the last Pacific-area exhibit at Chicago's Field Museum. For one thing, it displays only 500 or so artifacts from the Museum's Pacific Ocean collection of more than 55,000. (The last Pacific exhibit had between 5000 and 6000 artifacts on display for almost 60 years.) For another thing, it is a bright and often entertaining introduction to the area's geography, geology, biology, and anthropology. In 11,000 sq. ft., it shows how the Pacific islands were formed, how plants arrived, and how birds and other animals, including man, came to colonize them. It also offers a glimpse of how one or two islands look today. In an era when fewer than half of the nation's high school students can point out the 64 million square miles of the Pacific Ocean on a map, the exhibit is perhaps essential.

It concentrates on Micronesia, an area of atoll islands in the western tropical Pacific north of the equator. (A second phase of the permanent exhibit, concentrating on artifacts from other Pacific areas, opened a year later, in November 1990.) By the time Janet Kamien, chairman of the Field's design and production department, brought her staff into the project, it had been in the formative stages for a year. Design and production were to take three years more.

The exhibit greets visitors before they step through one of the many neoclassical arches, with which the Field frames its doorways, into the exhibit's first section. On the floor outside the arch, dark blue glazed-and-fired ceramic tiles

have been grouted to form a map of the Pacific (and the countries that ring it). The map is 18′ by 20′ with an oak border. Brown tiles form the land masses, while orange tiles represent the islands treated in the exhibit. Visitors can measure their foot size against a mileage scale on a wooden floor plaque, then walk off distances on the tile map. At one corner of the map, a fiberglass palm tree with vacuum-formed fronds arches 20′ overhead, growing out of a sand-sprinkled papier-mâché island.

Beyond the dark-blue-painted entrance arch, in a darkened room, is a 20′-by-20′ "lava flow" of cast fiberglass. Lighted from within by red lights shining through gaps in the fiberglass, the lava seems to move, as if devouring the road stripe painted on the floor; hissing recorded at a lava flow in Hawaii comes from internal speakers. On the lava is a 20″ video monitor playing a Hawaiian newscast about a lava flow.

In the next section, visitors see how the Pacific islands are formed. Above central models, illustrating stages in the formation of a volcanic island

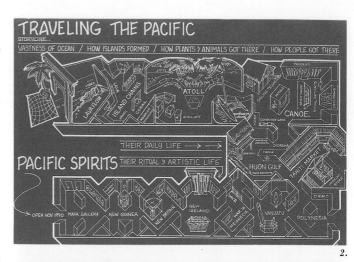

2.

1.

3.

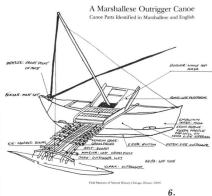

A Marshallese Outrigger Canoe
Canoe Parts Identified in Marshallese and English

chain, hangs (on cables from the ceiling) a 6'-by-12' map of the Hawaiian Islands, Midway, and the northern Pacific Rim islands of Kuril, Kamchatka, and the Aleutians. These are island chains that were formed by the lava as the earth's plates moved across hot spots on the ocean floor, and visitors can activate a mechanical model that uses a lava lamp—a psychedelic toy popular in Chicago in the '60s, in which a light bulb in a brass stand heats wax in a vial above it. As the wax heats up, it expands, releasing globules that rise to the surface something like oozing lava.

A reading rail snakes along the wall at waist height holding graphics and photos explaining how volcanoes rise from the sea floor to form islands. On the rail are lava samples that visitors can touch, and, in Plexi cases, plant and animal specimens with text explaining how they adapted to volcanic environments. The designers also used flappers—wood panels with questions screened on them that lift to reveal the answer. (Question: How hot is lava? Answer: 2000 degrees.)

In an introductory area for the section on the atoll is a 1'-

5.

1,3. Map of Pacific on floor tiles outside exhibit entrance. Visitors use their foot as a measure and step off distances.
2. Floor plan of both "Traveling the Pacific" and its companion exhibit "Pacific Spirits."
4. By turning crank, visitors activate rollers beneath a vinyl sheet, making the outrigger model undulate as if at sea.
5. Coral display. Visitors can look through magnifying glass and see difference between coral sand and Lake Michigan sand.
6. Drawing of outrigger.
7. Outrigger in place in exhibit diorama.

4.

7.

95/Exhibition Design

diameter chunk of coral. It is displayed free-standing on a waist-high wooden shelf between two 7′ columns of stacked glass blocks. In front of it, visitors can look through magnifying glasses to examine samples of coral sand from Hawaii and of quartz sand from Lake Michigan. Across the corridor-like space from this is a wall-mounted 300-gallon tank 7′ wide, 3′ high, and 2′ deep housing a small section of living coral reef and some of the animals that live with it.

This coral is a precursor of an 8′-deep curved diorama in two 35′-sections that re-creates an atoll in the Marshall Islands. The Field sent two expeditions to the Marshalls. One brought back latex, burlap, and blown foam castings taken of palm and pandanus trees. Hundreds of plants and thousands of leaves and flowers were also cast in resin or vacuum-formed styrene. Back at the Field, the museum staff hand-painted everything. A second expedition went after animals—birds, crabs, lizards, and snails. These were mounted in the diorama after taxidermy.

The diorama's first section is of the atoll's seaward side. Painted waves curl in on a sand beach. Background sound is of the waves, of palm fronds rustling, gulls crying. The second half depicts the atoll's calm lagoon side. Between the two diorama sections is a scale model (cast in polyester resin) of the two-mile-long atoll of which the diorama is a copy.

Across from the diorama, in one corner of this 2400-sq.-ft. area, the designers set up interactive devices. By pushing a plunger in a PVC tube,

visitors can create a wind that blows bits of Styrofoam over a three-dimensional diorama of islands, illustrating how the wind carries seeds to and through the islands. In yet another device, visitors can dunk a wire basket holding pandamus seeds and see that they float—another way that life spreads. Boxes (8″ by 8″) on top of a log from an atoll hold eggs, insects, and even a model fish to show how logs carry life from island to island.

In the corner opposite the interactive devices is the exhibit's centerpiece, a 20′-long Marshall Islands flexible outrigger canoe. Until it was shipped back to the Field by Phyllis Rabineau, who headed the exhibit's development team, the canoe had been sailing the waters of the Marshalls. Rabineau also sent two Marshallese men to Chicago to reassemble the canoe's outrigger and rigging. The exhibit designers set it on a beach re-created with sand and fiberglass palm trees and sea grapes against a wall mural of island, sea, and sky. Visitors peer at the canoe over a waist-high glass fence and read about canoe construction on text panels. Here, too, is an interactive model in which visitors can simulate the motion of an outrigger at sea. By turning a crank, visitors can put rollers in motion beneath a latex sheet on which an outrigger model undulates.

The same two Marshallese men who assembled the outrigger canoe thatched the pandamus roof of the canoe shed in the next section. The 12′-by-15′ shed, built with logs from Illinois and thatch from the

8.

9.

10.

8. Diorama recreates Marshall Island atoll.
9. Exhibit section explaining how lava forms islands. Through hole in box, visitor sees lava lamp, which simulates underground flow of lava.
10. Visitor feels two different types of lava.

11. Model of Huon Island house shows how islanders lived in 1910.
12. Recreation of contemporary Tahitian shops.
13. TV set riding a simulated lava flow plays news clips of real volcanic eruption.

Marshall Islands, fills one corner of the space and has a small canoe in it. In a central case are models of island canoes. A wall case 10′ by 9′ by 2′ and gently illuminated by 5-foot-candle spots protects vertically mounted paddles and other canoe artifacts in the Field's collection. Also in a central case is a 15′ ceremonial canoe, of a type that never goes to sea and is usually destroyed after the initiation ceremony in which it is used. Texts on free-standing case-high panels outside the cases and on waist-high tilted panels within the cases explain how islanders use canoes in their daily life.

In one corner of the space is a video booth with a bench for three or four persons to watch two 8-minute films, one of the initiation ceremony in Papua New Guinea in which islanders build a canoe, dance, and then break up the canoe with axes, and the other, of a contemporary canoe voyage made without instruments, following the stars and currents the way the ancients did, from Hawaii to New Zealand. Next to the video booth is a computer game in which visitors try to plan a canoe voyage to an uncharted island, estimating the requirements for success in terms of such things as food and water, numbers of people aboard, and time of year.

In its final two areas, the exhibit exposes visitors to two island locales—one from the past, one from the present. The first starts with a 9′-wide, 4′-deep diorama of a village in the Huon Gulf of Papua New Guinea as it was about 1910. Wall cases encircle the room with some of the thousands of

artifacts gathered long ago by the Field in the Huon Gulf. Wall-mounted, life-sized blowups show people using the artifacts. Also in the space are portions of two stilt houses, one a women's house, one a men's ceremonial house. The men's house has a 20′-long, 3′-wide plank carved with snakes and lizards and plants protected by a Plexiglas panel but used as siding in the house. A central case 10′ by 10′ by 4′ wide holds a canoe and fishing nets.

The exhibit's final area is an idealized version of a contemporary Tahitian market. Designed with the aid of hundreds of photographs of Papeete, Tahiti's central market, the 40′-by-50′ space includes shops (with housewares and fishing equipment) beneath an overhanging balcony and a central market in an aluminum truss-supported cage. Explaining the marketplace, Jeff Hoke, the Field's lead designer on the project, says: "The exhibit developers felt it important to engage the visitor in an environment shared by Pacific peoples today. Without it, we felt visitors could come away feeling that these were dead cultures, embalmed in the past." The Field's fabrication department built the village market with wood and tin from weathered northern Illinois farm buildings and with materials scrounged from three Chicago dumps.

Throughout the exhibit, lighting comes from fluorescent fixtures and ceiling spots pinpointing items on display.

The Field Musuem set aside 10 per cent of the $2,700,000 exhibit budget for revisions, to

11.

12.

13.

be guided by the suggestions of a professional evaluator once the exhibit's second phase opened. Already the designers know they will add more labels and interpretation in the lava section. They feel they need more footage of an actual lava flow.

Client: Field Museum of Natural History (Chicago, IL), Michael Spock, vice-president, public programs
Sponsors: Regenstein Foundation; National Endowment for the Humanities; National Endowment for the Arts; National Science Foundation; Chicago Park District
Design firm: Dept. of Exhibition, Field Museum of Natural History
Exhibit developers: Phyllis Rabineau (senior exhibit developer), Richard Faron, Robert Feldman, Robert Izor
Designers: Jeff Hoke, Paul Martin, Dianne Hanau-Strain, Lynn Hobbs, Mary Chiz
Consultants: People, Places and Design Research (evaluation); PML Exhibit Services (habitat design and fabrication); Field Museum curatorial staff and additional scientific advisors (content); Alele Museum of the Marshall Islands (habitat and canoe research); Harry Weese and Associates (architecture); Judy Rand (label writing); Musée de Tahiti et de Iles (marketplace)
Fabricators: Field Museum of Natural History production staff, Janet Kamien (chairperson), Tamara Biggs (project supervision); Dan Brinkmeier, Pat Guizzetti, Nancy Henriksson, Neil Keliher, Ray Leo, Mary Maxon (area leads)

The Living World

Ten thousand sq. ft. of exhibits at the St. Louis Zoo are a textbook of what late-20th-century exhibition design can do. Using almost all the technical devices currently available to exhibit designers, combining them with carefully thought out, imaginative graphics, photographs, and text, and mixing in a profusion of living animals, the designers present zoo visitors with what amounts to an introductory course in zoology and conservation. Although interactive video and computer devices arranged throughout the exhibit can make the "course" almost as detailed as a textbook (an entire biology textbook is, in fact, available on computers in the exhibit), it is also exuberant, rich, provocative, and fun. Part of the message is tough and direct: There are too many humans, the exhibit says, and we are raping the planet. If we don't stop—and it is already very late—mankind will not survive.

What the designers, the St. Louis architectural firm of Hellmuth, Obata and Kassabaum, wanted to create at the Living World was an exhibit that offered, according to Charles P. Reay, HOK senior vice-president and the exhibit's designer, "the best of education, the best of Disney,

and the best of the zoo." Reay developed and designed the exhibit in twin 4200-sq.-ft. exhibit halls located on two sides of the octagonal rotunda of the 55,000-sq.-ft. Wetterau Pavilion that HOK built to house the Living World, a two-level complex that includes exhibit space, theaters, classrooms, and offices. Reay produced 85 short films that play in the exhibit halls and in an adjacent theater. For four years, he worked on the project with an exhibit budget of $3,700,000.

Disney's influence is immediately evident to visitors who enter the exhibit on Living World's upper level in the May Company Hall—named "An Introduction to the Animals"—to the left of the 65'-high entry rotunda. Straight ahead, inside the animal hall's entrance, is Charles Darwin standing in a stage-set re-creation of his study. Darwin is a full-sized animatronic robot, the kind of figure the Disney organization originated for Disneyland. A computer guides his movements, compressed air drives his limbs, and his speech is recorded. He points to some live finches in a cage on his desk and to the exhibits in the room and says: "In this room is the greatest variety of animals under any roof in North America, or Britain for

that matter."

It was the designers' intent to show in this first of Living World's two octagonal exhibit halls the richness and diversity of animal life on earth. Flickering video screens, 5' across, 18 of them in the animal hall, play continuous 2½-minute video disk programs of animals going about their daily lives; "peep-shows," the designers call them. These screens are on the wall from 6½' to 9' off the floor. Beneath them, above a waist-high information rail, is a band of graphics and habitats for live animals, representing all the divisions of animal life. In all, this hall houses some 150 small species of animal life, arranged by their position in the animal kingdom, from one-celled organisms to mammals. These include sponges, corals, worms, starfish, insects, spiders, crabs, lobsters, salamanders, frogs, birds, fish, pigmy marmosets, squirrels, mice, and hamsters. Near the end is a full-sized model of an important mammal—Lucy, thought to be our first human ancestor. Overhead, suspended from the ceiling, is a 45'-long model of a giant squid.

Though most of the animals are in small (3' wide by 5' deep) natural habitats in the wall between the information rail and the video screens, some are in small boxes in the

rail itself. A segment of this rail runs 30" to 36" off the floor in front of each of the exhibit's sections. It is 14" wide with its Plexiglas top tilted toward the visitor at about 45 degrees. Its framing is 6"-diameter white oak, and its base is wood over a Unistrut system. The rails' bases house the computers, while the rails hold all the computer controls—keyboards, joysticks, touch screens. In addition, the rails hold graphics and metal boxes for small, live displays such as fruit flies or for fossils or insect collections. In many instances, fossils are shown in the rail beneath living specimens of the same animal, giving some idea of how the species evolved over millions of years.

Hellmuth, Obata and Kassabaum shaped the two exhibit halls especially for the exhibits. The 8-sided halls are identical, with walls rising 13½' to the roof spring point and the conical roof rising to a central peak of about 28'.

In the animal hall, exhibits ring the perimeter wall, divided into seven 22' sections, against each of the octagonal room's 28'-long walls. (The entrance is in the eighth segment.)

In the center of the animal hall is an octagonal island, ceiling-height, with eight walls measuring 8½' per side. It is against one of these walls that

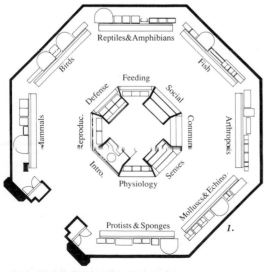

Introduction to the Animals

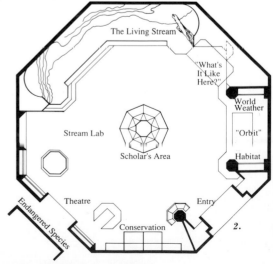

Introduction to Ecology

1,2. *Floor plans.*
3. *Architectural firm Hellmuth, Obata and Kassabaum designed both the building and the exhibits within it.*
4. *Building detail.*
5,6. *Central rotunda. Exhibit halls are on upper level.*

3.

5.

6.

Charles Darwin greets visitors. Set up in the same way as the exhibits on the perimeter, the exhibits on the interior island deal with physiology, blood temperature, and the senses. There is, for instance, a video game in which visitors listen to speakers emitting the noise of a flying moth. The moth appears on a video screen in front of them darting about a graveyard. Directed by the sound, game players must move a joystick on the rail to try to catch the moth. Above the screen are bats in a small habitat. On the rail are photos of bat faces, and on one of the 5′ overhead screens is a film segment of insectivorous bats in flight.

To illustrate how—despite their diversity—animals are basically alike, the designers isolated three things that all animals do: eat, reproduce, and defend themselves. An interactive video (with 1½ hours of material on each activity) shows the multitude of ways in which animals carry on each function.

Despite the welter of displays and devices, the animal hall's sound level is far from strident. All the peep shows (the 2½-minute videos of animals) and interactive screens use only images and text to get their messages across. Where Reay did call on sound was to support the animal theme. He filled the space with animal sounds which play from 20 speakers, but these sounds are muted and localized. They come from speakers aimed into parabolic disks that focus the sound at the floor. Each section has the sounds of the animals it displays (rain forest sounds in the ant habitat, for instance) and these

7.

8.

9.

10.

sounds can move around the hall. A fly will buzz from the insect area through the room; a flock of Canadian geese seems to fly over a broad area before settling into the bird section.

Reay prepared interactive material on sharks and birds. For the birds, he began by photographing the folio of Audubon's birds at the New York Historical Society. Using these images, the computer text tells about bird behavior: breeding, feeding, migrating, etc. When the computer is not in use, the screen shows a hand, supposedly Audubon's, painting a swan as soft harpsichord music plays.

Through the space along the wall above the animal aquariums and cases is an electronic time band which carries 25 minutes of information on the diversity of animal life. It tells of record sizes and actions—the longest migrations, for instance—and its motion and red lights draw people to it.

Across the rotunda from the animal hall is the other

octagonal exhibit hall—the McDonnell Douglas "An Introduction to Ecology." The two halls differ in more than location. Instead of the excitement of the animal hall with its flood of color and images—and its sound—the ecology hall is quiet, its pace slower, its mood more controlled and deliberate. Reay equates the two with yin and yang.

As visitors enter the ecology hall, they confront a movie in an area set off from the rest of the space by white columns. Pieced together from Landsat photographs, the 12-minute film is a high-definition video played on an 8′ screen of a satellite trip around the globe. It shows and discusses the earth's major habitats—the poles, deserts, savannahs, taigas (coniferous evergreen forests), rain forests. These habitats or niches become a springboard for exhibits showing how the earth's organisms are interconnected.

Reay sent out video crews to

11 major ecological regions (biomes) ranging from Barrow, Alaska, to Beliz in Central America. In each region, they sought what Reay calls shamans, old, wise persons connected to the land, and asked them three questions: What's it like here? What lives here? And what has changed in your lifetime? Back in St. Louis, the designers edited 11 hours of tape to one-and-a-half hours, put it on three video disks on three players and connected them to touch screens. To get information, visitors can touch a biome, touch a person, touch one of the questions, and so on.

The main display in the ecology hall is a 60′ re-creation of an Ozark mountain stream, along the outer wall, its water contained by a Plexiglas barrier. The species living in the stream are kept alive by halogen lamps with sun spectrum lights. Its plants are a mix of real and artificial. Its animals are the minnows, turtles, salamanders, frogs, turtles, plankton, and bass that live in Ozark streams.

In the rail in front of the stream, visitors can touch a computer screen to arbitrarily adjust populations and see what would happen. If they increase the number of bass, for instance, the plankton decrease, and so on.

In the center of the ecology hall is a scholars area with seats and eight interactive video screens. Six of these duplicate material from the exhibits, but here, visitors can sit and take their time looking things up. On laser disk is that complete biology textbook, and so is footage about current happenings in the zoo and in the animal world.

On the wall is a dot matrix display of world population that changes in jumps of 12 every 6 seconds. Beneath this is the number of species that have become extinct since 1989.

From the ecology hall, visitors go into the Requiem theater. Here, on three large screens, they watch a film conceived and produced by Chip Reay. Its images are of the

12.

13.

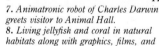

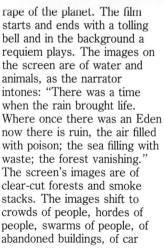

11.

14.

rape of the planet. The film starts and ends with a tolling bell and in the background a requiem plays. The images on the screen are of water and animals, as the narrator intones: "There was a time when the rain brought life. Where once there was an Eden now there is ruin, the air filled with poison; the sea filling with waste; the forest vanishing." The screen's images are of clear-cut forests and smoke stacks. The images shift to crowds of people, hordes of people, swarms of people, of abandoned buildings, of car

dumps. Clips from actual newscasts tell of oil spills, famine, tropical forest cutting. Then, in his newscast, Charles Kuralt points out that while men are the destroyers, they are also the carers. The film ends with Kuralt quoting Thoreau: "The earth is more to be admired than used. We need the tonic of wilderness. In wilderness is the preservation of the world." Finally, the images shift to those of flowers and frogs, zebra, monkeys, geese—and the sound; to a tolling bell.

7. *Animatronic robot of Charles Darwin greets visitor to Animal Hall.*
8. *Living jellyfish and coral in natural habitats along with graphics, films, and computer information fill this section of the Animal Hall.*
9. *Three-dimensional figures by cartoonist Ed Koren illustrate how animals communicate.*
10. *Cafeteria.*
11. *Overhead in Animal Hall is giant squid model. Note street-sign-like graphics that help guide visitors among displays in Animal Hall's central space.*
12. *Scholars' area in Ecology Hall has ecology and zoology information in computers, including a complete biology text.*
13. *Entrance to requiem theater in Ecology Hall. Crystal ball in foreground is habitat for colony of brine shrimp.*
14. *"Since You Were Born" display gives visitors printout of what's happened to planet since their arrival: species that have become extinct, tons of pollutants that have been added to atmosphere, etc.*

Client: St. Louis Zoo (St. Louis, MO)
Sponsors: Weterau, Inc.; Zoo Friends Association; Anheuser-Busch Charitable Trust; Southwestern Bell Foundation; Emerson Electric Co.; May Department Stores Co.; McDonnell Douglas Foundation & Employee Charity and Community Service; The Kresge Foundation; The Monsanto Fund; Apple Computer, Inc.; INTERCO, Inc. Charitable Trust; Boatmen's Bancshares; plus 2578 other donors
Design firm: Hellmuth, Obata & Kassabaum, Inc., St. Louis, MO
Designers: Charles P. Reay (director), Charles P. Reay, Jr., Bevin Grant (project designers)
Consultants: Dr. George Johnson (director, Living World), Dr. Peter Raven (director, Missouri Botanical Gardens, St. Louis)
Fabricators (exhibits): Crampton, Inc.; Larson Co.; New England Technology Group; Pierre Vacho; Oxford Scientific Films; David Rock; Holographics North; Ken Lieberman; Chuck Henderson; Sally Industries; Ed Koren; Bernie Krause; David Scharf; Sea Studios
Fabricators (graphics): Enameltec, Inc.; ASI Sign Systems; Amici, Inc.; Ridgewood Steel Fabricators; Signs, Letters, and Nameplates, Inc.; Bob Cassilly; Ken Lieberman

1.

O'Neill, a West Coast manufacturer of surfing wetsuits and sportswear, used this exhibit to grab attention at two trade shows, one in Long Beach, California, the other in Orlando, Florida.

O'Neill's initial problem was the same one facing anyone designing a trade show exhibit: how to be noticed in a sea of similar faces. O'Neill had not been satisfied with its past trade show performances, and for the first time the company turned the design of its exhibit space over to its in-house design arm, O'FX (O'Neill Effects International), which does all O'Neill's other design—from the product and its labels to advertising, brochures, and catalogs. Dave T. Parmley, who set up O'FX for O'Neill, and his staff took on the project with a confidence and enthusiasm that's evident in the outcome.

At Long Beach, O'Neill had the option of taking a central booth space on the open trade show floor or a much larger, 1100-sq.-ft., room at the rear of the hall, where they could ordinarily expect less traffic. Gambling on the larger, more remote, space, O'FX set about making it noticeable from anywhere on the floor.

First, they emphasized the O'Neill room and its entrance by erecting a logo of the O'Neill-sponsored surfing contest, the Coldwater Classic,

held in the company's home town, Santa Cruz, California. This logo, 25′ tall and 18′ wide, rose above the 8′-high, 12′-wide O'Neill room entrance. Sonotube columns at either side of the entrance were painted bright red with a paint textured with the roughest plaster wall compound they could find. These 8′-tall columns hid the entrance's outlines and seemed to support the giant logo overhead. From 40 yards away, O'FX suspended a 1000-watt spotlight from the ceiling grid some 30′ up and played it on the entrance logo.

Next, they set up a stack of 16 video monitors outside the entrance, to one side of the door. They put this stack (four rows of four screens) on a base that raised the middle horizontal rows of monitors to about eye level. Then they covered the base with what looked like red hot lava—or was supposed to. The lava came from cans of expandable foam sprayed on the plywood base and painted red.

O'Neill sponsors a team of surfers who race on the surfing circuit, and the O'FX designers made their own video to play on the monitor stack using clips of these surfers in action and in repose. Images of things like jet planes taking off were cut next to images of surfers taking off on waves and a soundtrack was put together of the surfers talking about big waves and surfing stunts. All of this, along with shots of O'Neill products and logos, was quick-cut and played by the computer in lively video-wall configurations. "We set the computer on random," says Dave Parmley, "and let it go."

Parmley, who has some

2.

3.

4.

5.

6.

7.

8.

9.

10.

1. Logo for O'Neill wetsuits and sportswear.
2-6. O'Neill advertising campaign uses Stay Boy, a skeletal dog.
7,8. Detail of photo blowups used in exhibit, showing O'Neill surfing team racers and logo.
9. Entrance to O'Neill trade show space with stack of TV screens and mechanical Stay Boy at right.
10. Sketch of TV stack.
11. Stay Boy growls at visitors.

11.

12.

13.

14.

digital audio equipment in his garage, spent several nights there with a friend and composed music for the soundtrack. With the video monitors flashing and the electronic sound booming from two big speakers, there was enough commotion to draw people to the O'Neill exhibit and hold them, at least until the 12-minute film sequences had played through.

O'Neill's space outside the entrance was 10′ by 30′ and sometimes there were as many as 30 or 40 persons standing around, spilling into the aisle, watching the video.

Across the entrance from the video stack were 12′ blowups of three of the O'Neill surfing team members. And right next to the monitors, between them and the entrance, was a 3′-high version of the "Stay Boy" dog, a mechanical manifestation of the dog that O'Neill uses in its advertising campaign and as the name of a design in its sportswear line. Parmley describes the exhibit's Stay Boy as "a hand-carved, mechanically articulated skeletal dog." His tail spun, his jaw snapped and his eyes (fitted with red motion bulbs) flickered. And, says Parmley, who, at home in his garage with his recording equipment, had done Stay Boy's voice, "he growled and grumbled," greeting visitors with remarks like "Your mother's a Chihuahua."

Inside was a blowup of the graphics for the "Aggression Is Our Obsession" line used in their ads plus more photo blowups (mounted on ½″ foamcore) of the O'Neill team (12′ high), one of the team in action (12′ by 18′), and of

models in O'Neill sportswear and of O'Neill logos. The space also held eight workstations with racks of O'Neill wetsuits and sportswear and, of course, tables for customers and salesmen. Colors were fluorescent, images chaotic.

The Casebook jurors called it "simple and punchy," and said the exhibit projected a "sense of what it was about."

O'FX put the show together, including fabrication, in 8 weeks.

15.

12-14. Interiór of O'Neill trade show space.
15. Stay Boy in chase.

Client: O'Neill (Santa Cruz, CA)
Design firm: O'FX (O'Neill Effects International), Santa Cruz, CA
Designers: Dave T. Parmley (art director), Mike Yankaus (assistant art director), Sandy Gin (senior designer), Kurt Parker, Sam Miranda, Michael Hernandez
Fabricator: O'FX